The Life and Times of
Akhnaton

Pharaoh of Egypt

BY

ARTHUR E. P. WEIGALL

CHIEF INSPECTOR OF THE DEPARTMENT OF ANTIQUITIES, UPPER EGYPT

AUTHOR OF 'A REPORT ON THE ANTIQUITIES OF LOWER NUBIA,' 'A CATALOGUE OF THE
WEIGHTS AND BALANCES IN THE CAIRO MUSEUM,' 'A GUIDE TO THE ANTIQUITIES
OF UPPER EGYPT,' 'DIE MASTABA DES GEMNIKAI' (WITH PROFESSOR VON
BISSING), 'TRAVELS IN THE UPPER EGYPTIAN DESERTS,' ETC.

ISBN: 978-1-63923-640-4

Printed: January 2023

Published and Distributed By:
Lushena Books
607 Country Club Drive, Unit E
Bensenville, IL 60106
www.lushenabks.com

ISBN: 9978-1-63923-640-4

TO

THEODORE M. DAVIS,

THE DISCOVERER OF
THE BONES OF AKHNATON,

𝔗𝔥𝔦𝔰 𝔅𝔬𝔬𝔨 𝔦𝔰 𝔇𝔢𝔡𝔦𝔠𝔞𝔱𝔢𝔡.

CONTENTS.

III.

AKHNATON FOUNDS A NEW CITY.

IV.

AKHNATON FORMULATES THE RELIGION OF ATON.

V.

THE TENTH TO THE TWELFTH YEARS OF THE REIGN OF AKHNATON.

VI.

THE THIRTEENTH TO THE FIFTEENTH YEARS OF THE REIGN OF AKHNATON.

VII.

THE LAST TWO YEARS OF THE REIGN OF AKHNATON.

VIII.

THE FALL OF THE RELIGION OF AKHNATON.

ILLUSTRATIONS.

"How much Akhnaton understood we cannot say, but he had certainly bounded forward in his views and symbolism to a position which we cannot logically improve upon at the present day."—PETRIE : 'History of Egypt.'

THE LIFE AND TIMES OF AKHNATON.

INTRODUCTION.

THE reign of Akhnaton, for seventeen years Pharaoh of Egypt (from B.C. 1375 to 1358), stands out as the most interesting epoch in the long sequence of Egyptian history. We have watched the endless line of dim Pharaohs go by, each lit momentarily by the pale lamp of our present knowledge, and most of them have left little impression upon the mind. They are so misty and far off, they have been dead and gone for such thousands of years, that they have almost entirely lost their individuality. We call out some royal name, and in response a vague

A

figure passes into view, stiffly moves its arms,
and passes again into the darkness. With one
there comes the muffled noise of battle; with
another there is singing and the sound of music;
with yet another the wailing of the oppressed
drifts by. But at the name Akhnaton there
emerges from the darkness a figure more clear
than that of any other Pharaoh, and with it
there comes the singing of birds, the laughter of
children, and the scent of many flowers. For
once we may look right into the mind of a king
of Egypt and may see something of its work-
ings; and all that is there observed is worthy
of admiration. Akhnaton has been called "the
first individual in human history";[1] but if he is
thus the first historical figure whose personality
is known to us, he is also the first of all human
founders of religious doctrines. Akhnaton may
be ranked in degree of time, and perhaps also in
degree of genius, as the world's first idealist;
and, since in all ancient Oriental research there
never has been, and probably never will be,

[1] Breasted : A History of Egypt.

brought before us a subject of such intellectual interest as this Pharaoh's religious revolution, which marks the first point in the study of advanced human thought, a careful consideration of this short reign deserves to be made.

The following pages do not pretend to do more than acquaint the reader with the subject, at a time when, owing to the recent discovery of the Pharaoh's bones, some interest may have been aroused in his career. A series of volumes have lately been issued by the Egypt Exploration Fund,[1] in which accurate copies are to be found of the reliefs, paintings, and inscriptions upon the walls of the tombs of some of Akhnaton's disciples and followers. In the year 1893 Professor Flinders Petrie excavated the site of the city which the Pharaoh founded, and published the results of his work in a volume entitled 'Tell el Amarna.'[2] Recently Professor J. H. Breasted has devoted some space to a masterly study of this period in his 'History of Egypt' and 'Ancient Records

---

[1] N. de G. Davies : The Rock Tombs of El Amarna. 5 vols.
[2] Now out of print.

of Egypt.'[1] From these publications the reader will be able to refer himself to the remaining literature dealing with the subject; but he should bear in mind that the discovery[2] of the bones of Akhnaton himself, which have shown us how old he was when he died — namely, about twenty-eight years of age,—have modified many of the deductions there made. Those who have travelled in Egypt will probably have visited the site of Akhnaton's city, near the modern village of El Amarna; and in the museums of Cairo, London, Paris, Berlin, Vienna, Leiden, and elsewhere, they will perhaps have seen some of the relics of his age.

During the last few years an extraordinary series of discoveries has been made in the Valley of the Tombs of the Kings at Thebes. In 1903 the tomb of Thothmes IV., the paternal grand-

---

[1] Published by the Chicago University, 1906.

[2] As will be recorded at the end of this volume, the body of Akhnaton was discovered by Mr Theodore M. Davis at Thebes early in 1907; but at the time of writing (1908) the results have not been published in book form, though various articles have appeared.

father of Akhnaton, was discovered; in 1905 the tomb of Yuaa and Tuau, the maternal grandparents of Akhnaton, was found; in 1907 Akhnaton's body was discovered in the tomb of his mother, Queen Tiy; and in 1908 the tomb of the Pharaoh Horemheb, one of the immediate successors of Akhnaton, was brought to light. At all but the first of these discoveries the present writer had the pleasure of assisting; and a particular interest in the period was thus engendered, of which the following sketch, prepared during an Upper-Egyptian summer, is an outcome. It must be understood, however, that a volume written at such times as the exigencies of official work allowed — partly in the shade of the rocks beside the Nile, partly at railway-stations or in the train, partly amidst the ruins of ancient temples, and partly in the darkened rooms of official quarters — cannot claim the value of a treatise prepared in an English study where books of reference are always at hand. It is hoped, however, that no errors have been made in the statement of the facts; and the deductions drawn therefrom are frankly open to the reader's criticism. There will certainly be no two opinions as to the acknowledgment of the originality, the power, and the idealism of the Pharaoh whose life is now to be outlined.[1]

[1] The writer has to thank the editors of 'The Quarterly Review,' 'Blackwood's Magazine,' and 'The Century Magazine,' for permitting him to embody in this volume certain portions of articles contributed by him to the pages of those journals.

I.

THE PARENTS AND GRANDPARENTS
OF AKHNATON.

---

1. THE ANCESTORS OF AKHNATON.

THE Eighteenth Dynasty of Egyptian kings took
possession of the throne of the Pharaohs in
the year 1580 B.C., over thirteen hundred
years after the buildings of the great pyramids,
and some two thousand years after the beginning
of dynastic history in the Nile Valley. The
founder of the dynasty was the Pharaoh
Aahmes I. He drove out the Asiatics who
had overrun the country during the previous
century, and pursued them into the heart of
Syria. His successor, Amonhotep I., penetrated as far as the territory between the
Orontes and the Euphrates; and the next

king, Thothmes I., was able to set his boundary - stone at the northern limits of Syria, and
thus could call himself the ruler of the entire
east end of the Mediterranean, the emperor
of all the countries from Asia Minor to the
Sudan. Thothmes II., the succeeding Pharaoh,
was occupied with wars in his southern dominions; but his successor, the famous Queen
Hatshepsut, was able to devote the years
of her reign to the arts of peace.

She was followed by the great warrior
Thothmes III., who conducted campaign after
campaign in Syria, and raised the prestige
of Egypt to a point never attained before
or after that time. Every year he returned
to Thebes, his capital, laden with the spoils
of Asia. From the capture of the city of
Megiddo alone he carried away 924 splendid
chariots, 2238 horses, 2400 head of various
kinds of cattle, 200 shining suits of armour,
including those of two kings, quantities of
gold and silver, the royal sceptre, the gorgeous
tent of one of the kings, and many minor
articles. Booty of like value was brought in
from other shattered kingdoms, and the Egyptian

treasuries were full to overflowing. The temples
of the gods also received their share of the
riches, and their altars groaned under the
weight of the offerings. Cyprus, Crete, and
perhaps the islands of the Ægean, sent their
yearly tribute to Thebes, whose streets, for
the first time in their history, were thronged
with foreigners. Here were to be seen the
long-robed Asiatics bearing vases fresh from
the hands of Tyrian craftsmen; here were
chariots mounted with gold and electrum
drawn by prancing Syrian horses; here were
Phœnician- merchants with their precious wares
stripped from the kingdoms of the sea; here
were negroes bearing their barbaric treasures
to the palace. The Egyptian soldiers held
their heads high as they walked through these
streets, for they were feared by all the world.
The talk was everywhere of conquest, and the
tales of adventure now related remained current
in Egypt for many a century. War-songs were
composed, and hymns of battle were inscribed
upon the temple walls. The spirit of the age
will be seen in the following lines, in which
the god Amon·addresses Thothmes III. :—

"I have come, giving thee to smite the princes of Zahi,
  I have hurled them beneath thy feet among their high-
    lands . . .
  Thou hast trampled those who are in the districts of Punt,
  I have made them see thy majesty as a circling star . . .
  Crete and Cyprus are in terror . . .
  Those who are in the midst of the great sea hear thy roarings ;
  I have made them see thy majesty as an avenger,
  Rising upon the back of his slain victim . . .
  I have made them see thy majesty as a fierce-eyed lion,
  While thou makest them corpses in their valleys . . ."

It was a fierce and a splendid age—the zenith
of Egypt's great history. The next king, Amonhotep II., carried on the conquests with a degree
of ferocity not previously apparent. He himself
was a man of great physical strength, who could
draw a bow which none of his soldiers could
use. He led his armies into his restless Asiatic
dominions, and having captured seven rebellious
Syrian, kings, he hung them head downwards
from the prow of his galley as he approached
Thebes, and later sacrificed six of them to Amon
with his own hand. The seventh he carried up
to a distant city of the Sudan, and there hung
him upon the gateway as a warning to all
rebels. Dying in the year 1420 B.C., he left the
throne to his son, Thothmes IV., the grandfather

of Akhnaton, who at his accession was about eighteen years of age.[1]

2. THE GODS OF EGYPT.

With the reign of Thothmes IV. we reach a period of history in which the beginnings are to be observed of certain religious movements, which become more apparent in the time of his son Amonhotep III. and his grandson Akhnaton. We must look, therefore, more closely at the events of this reign, and must especially observe their religious aspect. For this reason, and also in order that the reader may the more readily appreciate, by contrast, the pure teachings of the Pharaoh whose life forms the subject of the following pages, it will be necessary to glance at the nature of the religions which now held sway. Egypt had at this time existed as a civilised nation for over two thousand years, during the whole of which period these religious beliefs had been developing; and now they were so engrained in the hearts of the people that changes,

---

[1] Page 110.

however slight, assumed revolutionary proportions, requiring a master-mind for their initiation, and a hand of iron for their carrying into execution. At the time of which we now write, this mind and this hand had not yet come into existence, and the old gods of Egypt were at the zenith of their power.

Of these gods Amon, the presiding deity of Thebes, was the most powerful. He had been originally the tribal god of the Thebans, but when that city had become the capital of Egypt, he had risen to be the state god of the country. The sun-god Ra, or Ra-Horakhti, originally the deity of Heliopolis, a city not far from the modern Cairo, had been the state god in earlier times, and the priests of Amon contrived to identify the two deities under the name "Amon-Ra, King of the Gods." Amon had several forms. He was usually regarded as a man of shining countenance, upon whose head two tall feathers arose from a golden cap. Sometimes, however, he assumed the form of a heavy-horned ram. Sometimes, again, he adopted the appearance of a brother god, named Min, who was later identified with the Greek Pan; and it may be mentioned in passing that the goat-form of the Greek deity may have been derived from this Min-Amon of the Thebans. On occasions Amon would take upon himself the likeness of the reigning Pharaoh, choosing a moment when the monarch was away or was asleep, and in this manner he would obtain admittance to the queen's bed-chamber. Amonhotep III. himself was said to be the son of a union of this nature, though at the same time he did not deny that his earthly father was Thothmes IV. Amon delighted in battle, and gave willing assistance to the Pharaohs as they clubbed the heads of their enemies or cut their throats. It is possible that, like other of the Egyptian gods, he was but a deified chieftain of the prehistoric period whose love of battle had never been forgotten.

The goddess Mut, "the Mother," was the consort of Amon, who would sometimes come to earth to nurse the king's son at her breast. By Amon she had a son, Khonsu, who formed the third member of the Theban trinity. He was the god of the Moon, and was very fair to look upon.

Such were the Theban deities, whose influence upon the court was necessarily great. The Heliopolitan worship of the sun had also a very considerable degree of power at the palace. The god Ra was believed to have reigned as Pharaoh upon earth in the dim ages of the past, and it was thought that the successive sovereigns of Egypt were his direct descendants, though this tradition actually did not date from a period earlier than the Fifth Dynasty. "Son of the Sun" was one of the proudest titles of the Pharaohs, and the personal name of each successive monarch was held by him in the official titulary as the representative of Ra. While on earth Ra had had the misfortune to be bitten by a snake, and had been cured by the goddess Isis, who had demanded in return the revealing of the god's magical name. This was at last told her; but for fear that the secret would come to the ears of his subjects, Ra decided to bring about a general massacre of mankind. The slaughter was carried out by the goddess Hathor in her form of Sekhmet, a fierce lion-headed woman, who delighted to wade in streams of blood; but when only the half of mankind had

been slain, Ra repented, and brought the massacre to an end by causing the goddess to become drunk, by means of a gruesome potion of
blood and wine. Weary, however, with the cares
of state, he decided to retire into the heavens,
and there, as the sun, he daily sailed in his boat
from horizon to horizon. At dawn he was called
Khepera, and had the form of a beetle; at noon
he was Ra; and at sunset he took the name
of Atum, a word derived from the Syrian Adon,
"Lord," better known to us in its Greek translation "Adonis." As the rising and the setting
sun—that is to say, the sun near the horizon—
he was called Ra-Horakhti, a name which the
reader must bear in mind.

The goddess Isis, mentioned in the above
tradition, was the consort of Osiris, originally
a Lower Egyptian deity. Like Ra, this god
had also reigned upon earth, but had been
murdered by his brother Set, his death being
ultimately revenged by his son Horus, the
hawk. Thus Osiris, Isis, and Horus formed a
trinity, which at this time was mainly worshipped at Abydos, a city of Upper Egypt, where
it was thought that Osiris had been buried.

Having thus ceased to live upon earth, Osiris became the great King of the Underworld, and all persons prayed to him for their future welfare after death.

Meanwhile Horus, the hawk, was the tribal god of more than one city. At Edfu he was worshipped as the conqueror of Set; and in this manifestation he was the husband of Hathor, the lady of Dendereh, a city some considerable distance from Edfu. At Ombos, however, Set was worshipped, and in the local religion there was no trace of aught but the most friendly relations between Set and Horus. The goddess Hathor, at the same time, had become patron of the Western Hills, and in one of her earthly forms—namely, that of a cow—she is often seen emerging from her cavern in the cliffs.

At Memphis the tribal god was the little dwarf Ptah, the European Vulcan, the blacksmith, the artificer, and the potter of the gods. In this city also, as in many other districts of Egypt, there was a sacred bull, here called Apis, who was worshipped with divine honours and was regarded as an aspect of Ptah. At Elephantine a ram-headed deity named Khnum

was adored, and there was a sacred ram kept
in his temple for ceremonial purposes. As
Khnum had some connection with the First
Cataract of the Nile, which is situated near
Elephantine, he was regarded as of some importance throughout Egypt. Moreover, he was
supposed by some to have used the mud at the
bottom of the Nile to form the first human
being, and thus he found a place in the mythology of several districts.

A vulture, named Nekheb, was the tribal
deity of the trading city of Eileithiaspolis; a
ferocious crocodile, Sebek, was the god of a
second city of the name of Ombos; an ibis,
Thoth, was that of Hermopolis; a cat, Bast,
that of Bubastis; and so on—almost every city
having its tribal god. Besides these there were
other more abstract deities: Nut, the heavens,
who, in the form of a woman, spread herself
across the sky; Seb, the earth; Shu, the vast-
ness of space; and so forth. The old gods of
Egypt were indeed a multitude. Here were
those who had marched into the country at
the head of conquering tribes; here were
ancient heroes and chieftains individually dei-

fied, or ˏoften identified with the god whom
their tribe had served; here were the elements
personified; here the orbs of heaven which
man could see above him. As intercourse
between city and city became more general,
one set of beliefs had been brought into line
with another, and myths had developed to
explain the discrepancies. Thus in the time
of Thothmes IV. the heavens were crowded
with gods; but standing above them all, the
reader will do well to familiarise himself with
the figure of Amon-Ra, the god of Thebes,
and with Ra-Horakhti, the god of Heliopolis.
In the following pages the lesser denizens of
the Egyptian Olympus play no great part, save
as a routed army hurled back into the ignorant
darkness from which they came.

3. THE DEMIGODS AND SPIRITS—THE PRIESTHOODS.

The sacred bulls and rams mentioned above
were relics of an ancient animal-worship, the
origin of which is lost in the obscurity of pre-

history.   The Egyptians paid homage to a variety
of animals, and almost every city or district
possessed its particular species to which special
protection was extended.   At Hermopolis and
in other parts of Egypt the baboon was sacred,
as well as the ibis, which typified the god Thoth.
Cats were sacred both at Bubastis, where the cat-
goddess, Bast, resided, and in various other districts.   Crocodiles were very generally held in
reverence, and several river fish were thus
treated.   The snake was much feared and
reverenced; and, as a pertinent example of this
superstition, it may be mentioned that Amonhotep III., the father of Akhnaton, placed a
figure of the agathodemon serpent in a temple
at Benha.   The cobra was reverenced as the
symbol of Uazet, the goddess of the Delta, and,
first used as a royal emblem by the archaic
kings of that country, it became the main
emblem of sovereignty in Pharaonic times.   It
is unnecessary here to look more closely at this
aspect of Egyptian religion; and but a word
need be said of the thousand demons and spirits
which, together with the gods and the sacred
animals, crowded the regions of the unknown.

Many were the names which the magician might
call upon in the hour of his need, and many
were the awful forms which the soul of a man
who had died was liable to meet. Osiris, the
great god of the dead, was served by four such
genii, and under his authority there sat no less
than forty-two terrible demons whose business
it was to judge the quavering soul. The
numerous gates of the underworld were guarded
by monsters whose names alone would strike
terror into the heart, and the unfortunate soul
had to repeat endless and peculiarly tedious
formulæ before admittance was granted.

To minister to these hosts of heaven there
had of necessity to be vast numbers of priests.
At Thebes the priesthood of Amon formed an
organisation of such power and wealth that the
actions of the Pharaoh had largely come to be
controlled by it. The High Priest of Amon-Ra
was one of the most important personages in
the land, and his immediate subordinates, the
Second, Third, and Fourth Priests, as they were
called, were usually nobles of the highest rank.
The High Priest of Amon was at this period
often Grand Vizir also, and thus combined the

highest civil appointment with the highest
sacerdotal office. The priesthood of Ra at
Heliopolis, although of far less power than that
of Amon, was also a body of great importance.
The High Priest was known as "the Great
One of Visions," and he was probably less of a
politician and more of a priest than his Theban
colleague. The High Priest of Ptah at Memphis
was called "the Great Master Artificer," Ptah
being the Vulcan of Egypt. He, however, and
the many other high priests of the various gods,
did not rank with the two great leaders of the
Amon and the Ra priesthoods.

4. THOTHMES IV. AND MUTEMUA.

When Thothmes IV. ascended the throne he
was confronted by a very serious political prob-
lem. The Heliopolitan priesthood at this time
was chafing against the power of Amon, and
was striving to restore the somewhat fallen
prestige of its own god Ra, who in the far
past had been the supreme deity of Egypt, but
had now to play an annoying second to the

Theban god. Thothmes IV., as we shall
presently be told by Akhnaton himself,[1] did
not altogether approve of the political character
of the Amon priesthood, and it may have been
due to this dissatisfaction that he undertook
the repairing of the great sphinx at Gizeh,
which was in the care of the priests of Heliopolis.   The sphinx was thought to represent a
combination of the Heliopolitan gods Horakhti,
Khepera, Ra, and Atum, who have been
mentioned above; and, according to a later
tradition, Thothmes IV. had obtained the throne
over the heads of his elder brothers through
the mediation of the sphinx — that is to say,
through that of the Heliopolitan priests.   By
them he was called " Son of Atum and Protector
of Horakhte, . . . who purifies Heliopolis and
satisfies Ra,"[2] and it seems that they looked
to him to restore to them their lost power.   The
Pharaoh, however, was a physical weakling, whose
small amount of energy was entirely expended
upon his army, which he greatly loved, and
which he led into Syria and into the Sudan.
His brief reign of somewhat over eight years,

---

[1] Page 100.   [2] The sphinx tablet.

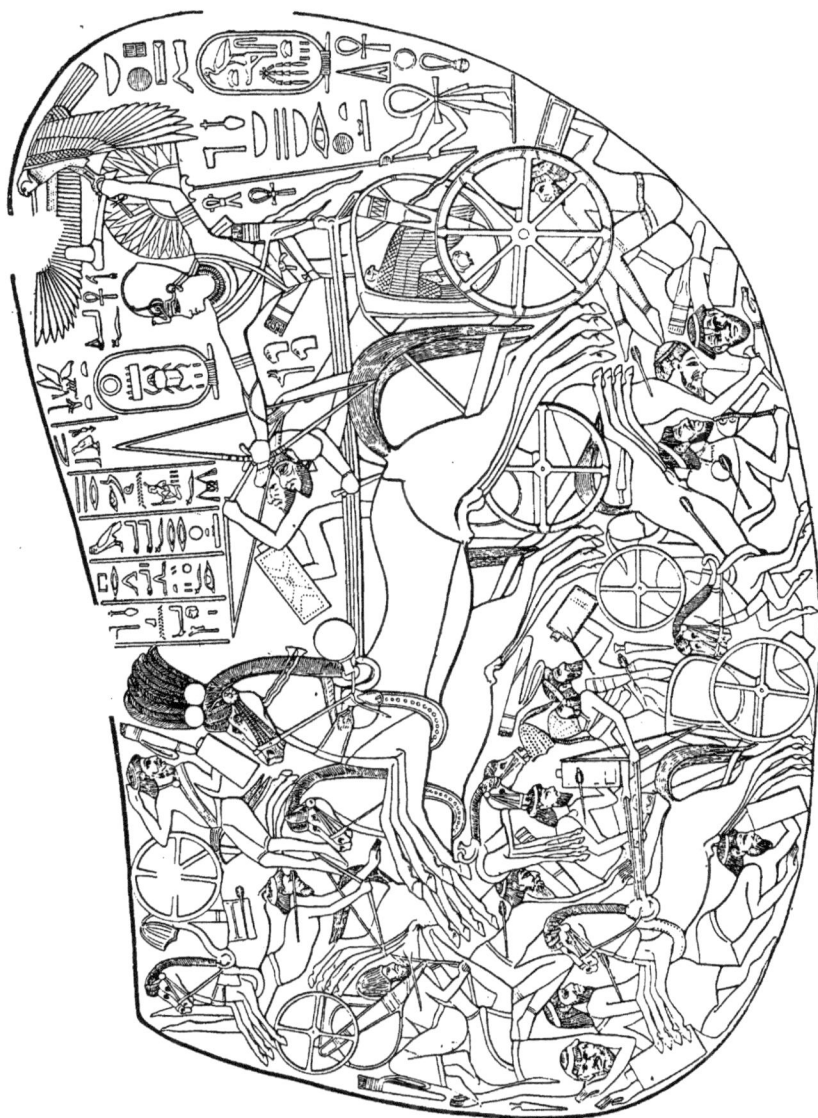

Thothmes IV. slaying Asiatics.

from 1420 to 1411 B.C., marks but the indecisive beginnings of the struggle between Amon and Ra, which culminated in the early years of the reign, of his grandson Akhnaton.

Some time before he came to the throne he had married a daughter of the King of Mitanni, a North - Syrian state which acted as a buffer between the Egyptian possessions in Syria and the hostile lands of Asia Minor and Mesopotamia, and which it was desirable, therefore, to placate by such a union. There is little doubt that this princess is to be identified with the Queen Mutemua, of whom several monuments exist, and who was the mother of Amonhotep III., the son and successor of Thothmes IV. A foreign element was thus introduced into the court which much altered its character, and led to numerous changes of a very radical nature. It may be that this Asiatic influence induced the Pharaoh to give further encouragement to the priest of Heliopolis. The god Atum, the aspect of Ra as the setting sun, was, as has been said, of common origin with Aton or Adonis, who was largely worshipped in North Syria ; and the foreign queen with her retinue may have therefore felt more sympathy with Heliopolis than with Thebes. Moreover, it was the Asiatic tendency to speculate in religious questions, and the doctrines of the priests of the northern god were more flexible and more adaptable to the thinker than was the stiff, formal creed of Amon. Thus, the foreign thought which had now been introduced into Egypt, and especially into the palace, may have contributed somewhat to the dissatisfaction with the state religion which becomes apparent during this reign.

Very little is known of the character of Thothmes IV., and nothing which bears upon that of his grandson Akhnaton is to be ascertained. Although of feeble health and unmanly physique, he was a fond upholder of the martial dignity of Egypt. He delighted to honour the memory of those Pharaohs of the past who had achieved the greatest fame as warriors. Thus he restored the monuments of Thothmes III., of Aahmes I., and of Senusert III.,[1] the three greatest military leaders of Egyptian history. As a decoration for his chariot there were scenes

---

[1] Of Thothmes III. at Karnak, of Aahmes I. at Abydos, and of Senusert III. at Amada.

representing him trampling upon his foes; and
when he died many weapons of war were buried
with him. Of Queen Mutemua's character
nothing is known; and the attention of the
reader may at once be carried on to Akhnaton's
maternal grandparents, the father and mother
of Queen Tiy.

5. YUAA AND TUAU.

Somewhere about the year 1470 B.C., while the
great Thothmes III. was campaigning in Syria,
the child was born who was destined to become
the grandfather of the most remarkable of all
the Pharaohs of Egypt. Neither the names of
the parents nor the place of birth are known;
and the reader will presently find that it is not
easy to say whether the child was an Egyptian
or a foreigner. His name is written Aau, Aay,
Aai, Ayu, A-aa, Yaa, Yau, and most commonly
Yuaa; and this variety of spelling seems rather
to indicate that its pronunciation, being foreign,
did not permit of a correct rendering in Egyptian
letters. He must have been some twenty years
of age when Thothmes III. died; and thus it is

quite possible that he was one of those Syrian princes whom the Pharaoh brought back to Egypt from the courts of Asia to be educated in the Egyptian manner. Some of these hostages who were not direct heirs to Syrian thrones may have taken up their permanent residence on the banks of the Nile, where it is certain that a fair number of their countrymen were settled for business and other purposes. During the reign of Amonhotep II., Yuaa must have passed the prime years of his life, and at that king's death he had probably reached about the forty-fifth year of his age. He had married a woman called by the common Egyptian name of Tuau, regarding whose nationality there is, therefore, not much question. Two children were born of the marriage, the first a boy who was named Aanen, and the second a girl named Tiy, who later became the great queen. Tiy was probably a little girl some two years old when Thothmes IV. came to the throne, and as her parents both held appointments at court, she must have presently received those first impressions of royal luxury which influenced her childhood and her whole life.

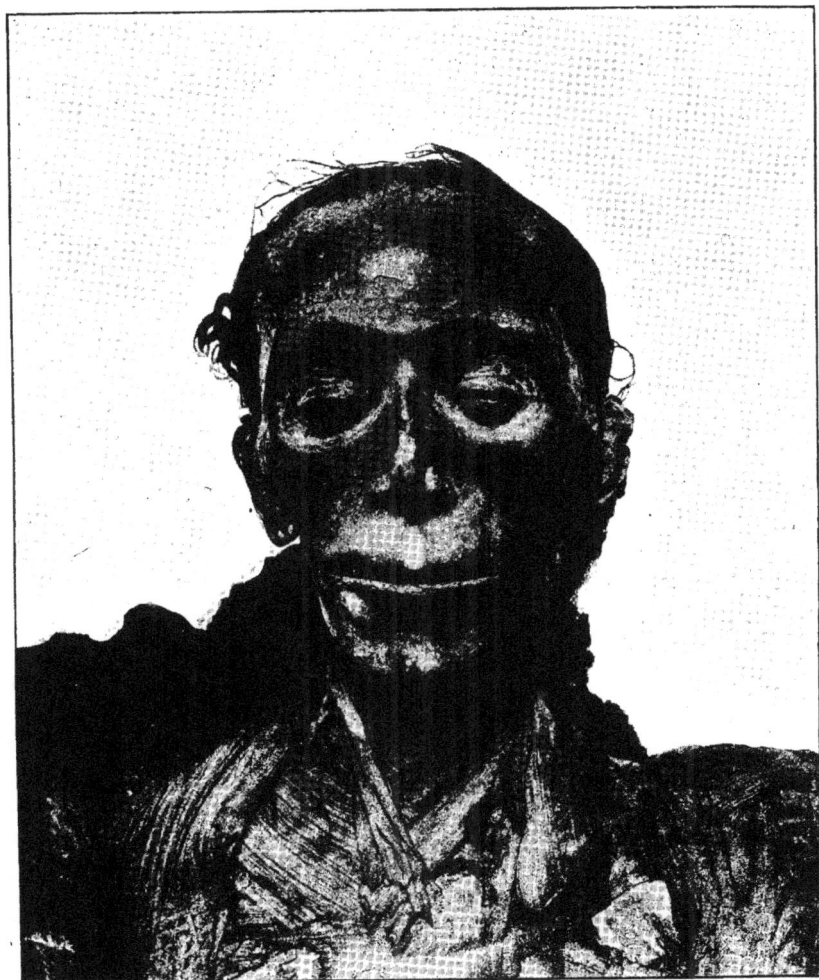

Tuau, grandmother of Akhnaton.

At this time Yuaa held the sacerdotal office of Priest of Min, one of the most ancient of the Egyptian gods. Min, who had many of the characteristics of, and was later identified with, the Greek Pan, was worshipped at three or four cities of Upper Egypt, and throughout the Eastern Desert to the Red Sea coast. He was the god of fecundity, fertility, generation, reproduction, and the like, in the human, animal, and vegetable worlds. In his form of Min-Ra he was a god of the sun, whose fertilising rays made pregnant the whole earth. He was more noble than the Greek Pan, and represented the pristine desires of lawful reproduction in the family, rather than the erotic instincts for which the Greek god was famous. Were one to compare him with any of the gods of the countries neighbouring to Egypt, he would be found to have as much likeness to the above-mentioned Adonis, who in North Syria was a god of vegetation, as to any other deity. This fact offers food for some thought, for if Yuaa was a foreigner, hailing, as may be supposed, from Syria, there would have been no Egyptian god, except Atum, to whose service he would have attached himself

so readily as to that of Min. Although a tribal
god, Min was not essentially the protector and
upholder of Egyptian rights and Egyptian pre-
judices. He was, in one form or another, universal; and he must have appealed to the sense
and the senses of Syrian and Egyptian alike.

At this time, as we have seen, the priests of
Amon, whose wealth had brought corruption in
its train, were under the cloud of royal dis-
pleasure, and the court was beginning to display a desire to rid itself of an influence which
was daily becoming less exalted. It may be
that Yuaa, upholding the doctrines of Min and
of Adonis, had some connection with this movement, for he was now a personage of considerable importance at the palace. He may have
already held the title of Prince or Duke, by
which he is called in his funeral inscriptions;
and one may suppose that he was a favourite
of the young king, Thothmes IV., and of his
wife, Queen Mutemua, whose blood was soon
to unite with his own in the person of Akhnaton.
When Thothmes IV. died at the age of twenty-
six, and his son Amonhotep III., a boy of
twelve years of age, came to the throne, Yuaa

Chest belonging to Yuaa.

was a man of over fifty, and his little daughter
Tiy was a girl of marriageable age according
to Egyptian ideas, being about ten years old.[1]

The court at this time was more or less under
the influence of the now Queen-Regent Mutemua
and her advisers, for Amonhotep III. was still
too young to be allowed to go entirely his own
way, and amongst those advisers it seems evident
that Yuaa was to be numbered. Now the boy-
king had not been on the throne more than a
year, if as much, when, with feasting and ceremony, he was married to Tiy; and Yuaa and
Tuau became the proud parents-in-law of the
Pharaoh.

It is necessary to consider the significance of
the marriage. The royal pair were the merest
children; and it is impossible to suppose that
the marriage was not arranged for them by
their guardians. If Amonhotep at this early
age had simply fallen in love with this girl,
with whom probably he had been brought up,
he, no doubt, would have insisted on marrying
her, and she would have been placed in his
harîm. But she became his Great Queen, was

---

[1] These ages are discussed on pages 111 and 178 (note).

placed on the throne beside him, and received
honours which no other queen of the most
royal blood had ever received before.   It is
clear that the king's advisers would never have
permittèd this had Tiy been but the pretty
daughter of a noble of the court.   There must
have been something in her parentage which
entitled her to these honours and caused her
to be chosen deliberately as queen.

There are several possibilities.   Tuau may have
had royal blood in her veins, and may have been,
for instance, the granddaughter of Thothmes
III., to whom she bears some likeness in face.
Queen Tiy is often called " Royal Daughter " as
well as " Royal Wife "; and it is possible that
this is to be taken literally.   In a letter sent by
Dushratta, King of Mitanni, to Akhnaton, Tiy is
called " my sister and thy mother "; and though
it is possible that the word " sister " is here used
to indicate the general cousinship of royalty, it
is more probable that some real connection is
meant, for other relationships, such as " daughter,"
" wife," and " father-in-law," are precisely stated
in the letter.   Yuaa may have been indirectly
of royal Egyptian blood, or he may have been,

Queen Tiy.

as we have seen, the offspring of some Syrian royal
house, such as that of Mitanni, related by marriage
with the Pharaoh ; and thus Tiy may have had
some distant claim to the throne, and Dushratta
would have had reason for calling her his sister.
Queen Tiy, however, has so often been called a
foreigner for reasons which have now been shown
to be quite erroneous that we must be cautious in
adopting any of these possibilities. It has been
stated that her face is North-Syrian in type,[1] and,
as the portrait upon which this statement is based
is, in all features except the nose, reminiscent of
Yuaa, that noble would also resemble the people
of that country ; and in this connection it must
be remembered that the marriage of Tiy and
Amonhotep took place under the regency of
Mutemua, herself probably a North - Syrian
princess. Be this as it may, however, the two
children, not yet in their 'teens, ruled Egypt

---

[1] Petrie, History, ii. p. 183. The portrait upon which he bases
this statement, however, may be that of Akhnaton (fig. 115, p.
182). The mouth and chin are extremely like those of Yuaa, as
seen in his mummy ; but again they both have a close resemblance
to the head of Amonhotep III. (*idem*, fig. 120, p. 188). Of course,
such evidence is extremely frail, and must not be too much relied
upon.

together, and Yuaa and Tuau stood behind the throne to advise them.

Tuau now included amongst her titles those of "Royal Handmaid," or lady - in - waiting, "the favoured-one of Hathor," "the favourite of the King," and "the Royal mother of the great wife of the King," a title which may indicate that she was of royal blood. Amongst the titles of Yuaa one may mention those of "Master of the Horse and Chariot-Captain of the King," "the favourite, excellent above all favourites," and "the mouth and ears of the King,"—that is to say, his agent and adviser. He was a personage of commanding presence, whose powerful character showed itself in his face. One must picture him now as a tall man, with a fine shock of white hair; a great hooked nose, like that of a Syrian; full, strong lips; and a prominent, determined jaw. He has the face of an ecclesiastic, and there is something about his mouth which reminds one of the late Pope, Leo XIII. One feels, in looking at his well-preserved features, that here perhaps may be found the originator of the great religious movement which his daughter and grandson carried into execution.

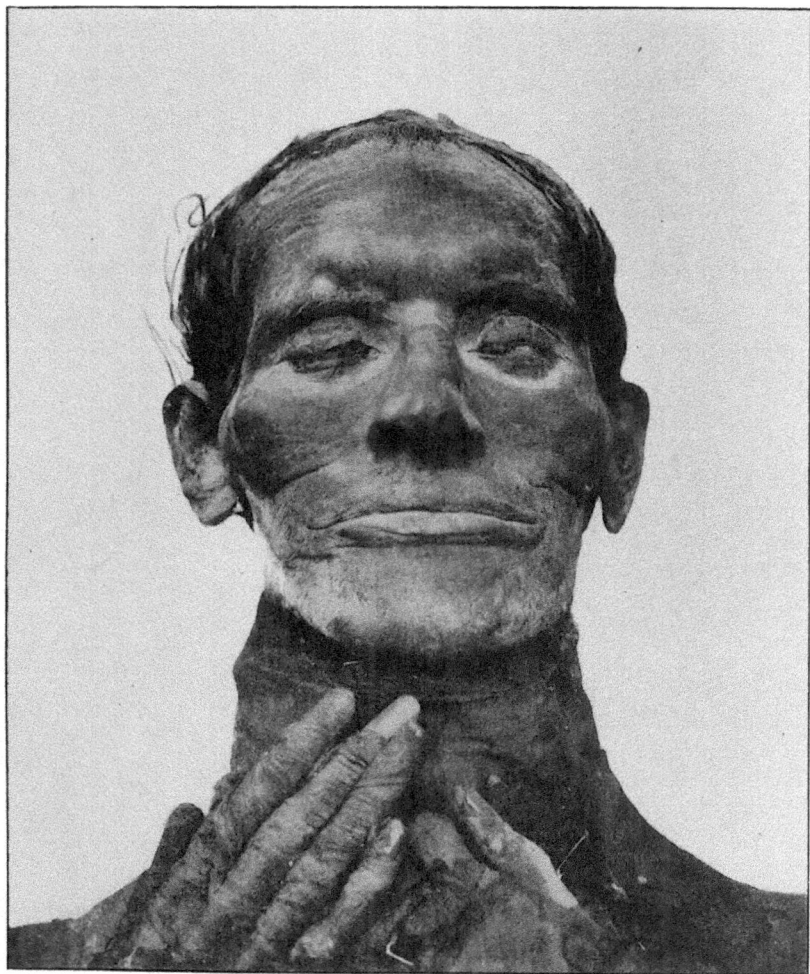

Yuaa, grandfather of Akhnaton.

6. AMONHOTEP III. AND HIS COURT.

Besides Yuaa and Tuau and the Queen-Dowager Mutemua, there was a certain noble, named Amonhotep-son-of-Hapu, who may have exercised considerable influence upon the young Pharaoh. So good and wise a man was he, that in later times he was regarded almost as a divinity, and his sayings were treasured from generation to generation. It may be that he furthered the cause of the Heliopolitan priesthood against that of Amon; and it is to be observed in this connection that, in the inscription engraved upon his statue, he refers to the Pharaoh as the "heir of Atum" and the "first-born son of Horakhti," those being the Heliopolitan gods. When, presently, a daughter was born to Tiy, who was named Setamon, this philosopher was given the honorary post of "Steward" to the princess; while at the same time he filled the office of Minister of Public Works, and held various court appointments. At this period, when religious speculation was beginning to be freely indulged in, the influence

of a "wise man" of this character would necessarily be great; and should any of his sayings
come to light, they will perhaps be found to
bear upon the subject of the religious changes
which were now taking place. A late tradition
tells us that this Amonhotep had warned the
Pharaoh that if he would see the true God he
must drive from his kingdom all impure persons;
and herein one may perhaps observe some reference to the corrupt priests of Amon, whose
ejection from their offices was daily becoming
more necessary.

At the time of which we write Egypt still
remained at that height of power to which the
military skill of Thothmes III. had raised her.
The Kings of Palestine and Syria were tribu-
taries to the young Pharaoh; the princes of the
sea-coast cities sent their yearly impost to
Thebes; Cyprus, Crete, and even the Greek
islands, were Egyptianised; Sinai and the Red
Sea coast as far south as Somaliland were included in the Pharaoh's dominions; and the
negro tribes of the Sudan were his slaves. Egypt
was indeed the greatest state in the world, and
Thebes was a metropolis at which the ambas-

Amonhotep-son-of-Hapu, the "wise man," of the
Court of Amonhotep III.

sadors, the merchants, and the artisans from
these various countries met together. Here
they could look upon buildings undreamed of
in their own lands, and could participate in
luxuries unknown even in Babylon. The wealth
of Egypt was so enormous that a foreign sovereign
who wrote to the Pharaoh asking for gold
mentioned that it could not be considered as
anything more valuable than so much dust by
an Egyptian. Golden vases in vast quantities
adorned the tables of the king and his nobles,
and hundreds of golden vessels of different kinds
were used in the temples.

The splendour and gaiety of the court at
Thebes remind one of the tales from the Arabian
Nights. One reads of banquets, of splendid
festivals on the water, of jubilee celebrations,
and of hunting parties. When the scenes depicted on the monuments are gathered together
in the mind, and the ruins which are left are
there reconstructed, a life of the most intense
brilliancy is shown. This was rather a development of the period than a condition of things
which had been derived from an earlier *régime.*
The Egyptians had always been a happy, light-

hearted people; but it was the conquests of
Thothmes III. that had given them the security
and the wealth to live as luxuriously as they
pleased. The tendency of the nation was now
to break away from the old, hardy traditions of
the earlier periods of Egyptian history; and
virtually no other body, except the priesthood
of Amon, held them down to ancient conventionalities. But while the king and his court
made merry and amused themselves in sumptuous
fashion, that god Amon and his representatives
towered over them like some sombre bogie, holding them to a religion which they considered to be
obsolete, and claiming its share of royal wealth.

About the time of his marriage Amonhotep
built a palace on the western bank of the Nile,
on the edge of the desert under the Theban
hills, and here Queen Tiy held her brilliant
court. The palace was a light but roomy structure of brick and costly woods, exquisitely decorated with paintings on stucco, and embellished
with delicate columns. Along one side ran a
balcony on which were rugs and many-coloured
cushions, and here the king and queen could
sometimes be seen by their subjects. Gardens

CEILING DECORATION FROM THE PALACE OF AMONHOTEP III.

surrounded the palace, almost at the gates of which rose the splendid hills. On the eastern side of the building the king later constructed a huge pleasure-lake especially for the amusement of Tiy. The mounds of earth which were thrown up during its excavation were purposely formed into irregular hills, and these were covered with trees and flowers. Here the queen floated in her barge, which, in honour of the Heliopolitan god, she called "Aton-gleams"; and as she watched the reflections of the hills and the trees in the still water, she may well have imagined herself in those fair lands of Syria from which Aton or Adonis had come.

The name Aton was Syrian. The setting sun, as we have seen, was called in Egypt Atum, which was derived from the Asiatic Adon or Aton; and it is now that we first find the word introduced into Egypt as a synonym of Ra-Horakhti - Khepera - Atum of Heliopolis. Presently we find that one of the Pharaoh's regiments of soldiers is named after this god Aton, and here and there the word now occurs upon the monuments. Thus, gradually, the court was bringing a new-named deity into prominence, closely related to the gods of Heliopolis; and it may be supposed that the priesthood of Amon watched the development with considerable perturbation. The Pharaoh himself does not seem to have worried very considerably with regard to these religious matters. He was, it seems, a man addicted to pleasure, whose interests lay as much in the hunting-field as in the palace. He loved to boast that during the first ten years of his reign he had slain 102 lions; but as he was a mere boy when he first indulged in this form of sport, it is to be presumed that his nobles assisted him handsomely in the slaughter on each occasion. In one day he is reported to have killed fifty-six wild cattle, and a score more fell to him a few days later; but here again one may suppose that the glory and not the deed was his.

In the fifth year of his reign he led an expedition into the Sudan to chastise some tribe which had rebelled, and he records with pride the slaughter which he had made. It is stated that these negroes "had been haughty, and great things were in their hearts; but the fierce-eyed lion, this prince, he slew them by the command

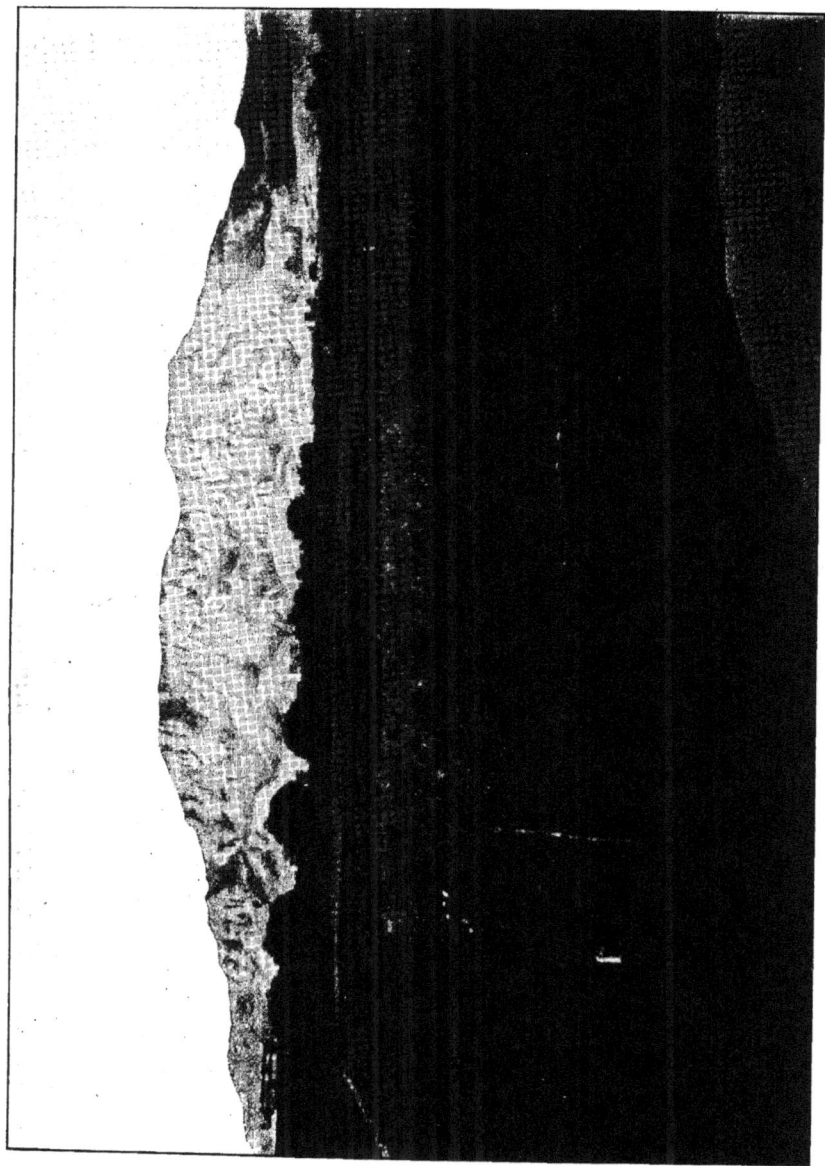

Site of the Palace of Queen Tiy.

of Amon-Atum." It is interesting to notice that Atum is thus brought into equal prominence with Amon, and one may see from this the trend of public opinion.

At this time the Vizir, a certain Ptahmes, held also the office of High Priest of Amon; but when he died he was not succeeded in his duties as Vizir by the new head of the Amon priesthood, as was to be expected. The Pharaoh appointed a noble named Rames as his prime minister, and thus separated the civil and the religious power : a step which again shows us something of the movement which was steadily diminishing the power of Amon.

Queen Tiy seems to have borne several daughters to the king, and it is possible that she had also presented him with a son. But, if this is so, he had died in early childhood, and no heir to the throne was now living. It may have been partly due to this fact that Amonhotep, in the tenth year of his reign, married the Princess Kirgipa or Gilukhipa, daughter of the King of Mitanni, and probably niece of the Dowager-Queen Mutemua.[1] The princess came to Egypt

---

[1] Breasted, Records, ii. 865, note h.

in considerable state, bringing with her 317
ladies-in-waiting; but she seems to have been
thrust into the background by Tiy, who, even
in the official record of the marriage, is called
the king's chief wife. The marriage may have
been purely political, as was that of Thothmes
IV.; and there is certainly no record of any
children born to Gilukhipa. She and her ladies
but added a further foreign element to the life
of the palace, and swelled the numbers of those
who had no sympathy with the old gods of
Thebes.

It must have been somewhere about the year
1390 B.C. that Tiy's aged father, Yuaa, died;
and Tuau soon followed him to the grave. They
were buried in a fine sepulchre in the Valley
of the Tombs of the Kings at Thebes; and if
they are not to be considered as royal, this will
have been the first time that persons not of
royal blood had been buried in a tomb of large
size in this valley. A quantity of funeral furniture
was placed around the splendid coffins in which
their mummies lay, and amongst this there were
a few objects which evidently had been presented by the bereaved king and queen and by

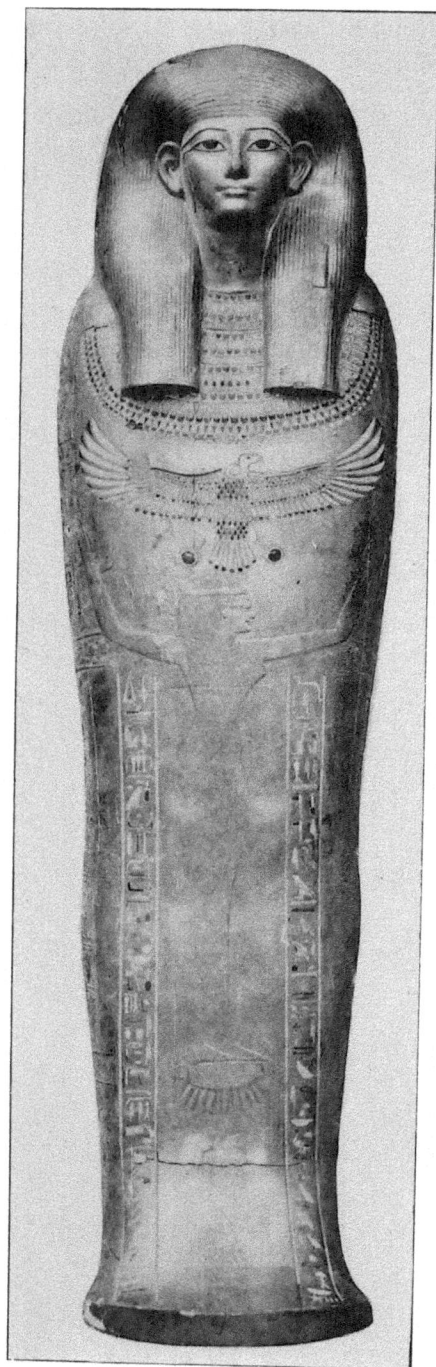

Coffin of Yuaa.

the young princesses, Setamon and another whose
name is now lost. Yuaa and his wife had evidently been much beloved at the court, and as
the parents of the great queen they had com-
manded the respect of all men. To us they are
remarkable as the grandparents of that great
teacher, Akhnaton, whose birth has now to be
recorded.

II.

THE BIRTH AND EARLY YEARS OF AKHNATON.

1. THE BIRTH OF AKHNATON.

IT has been seen that Queen Tiy presented several children to the king; but it was not until they had reigned some twenty - five or twenty-six years that the future monarch was born. As the years had passed the queen must have grown more and more anxious for a son, and many must have been the prayers she offered up that a male child might be vouchsafed to her. In Egypt at the present day the desire to bear a son holds dominion in the heart of every young woman; and those to whom this privilege has not been granted forsake the laws of the prophet and still lay their passionate

appeal before the old gods. The present writer
was asked recently by a young peasant to allow
his wife to walk round the outer wall of an
ancient temple, in order that she might per-
chance bear a male child thereafter; and on another occasion three young women were seen
sliding down the plinth of an overturned statue
of Rameses the Great for the same purpose.
With similar emotion, though with greater intel-
ligence, Queen Tiy must have turned in her grief
from one god to another, promising them all
manner of gifts if they would grant her desire.
To Ra - Horakhti Aton she appears to have
turned with the most confidence; and perhaps,
as will presently be seen, she vowed that if a
son were granted to her she would dedicate him
to the service of that god.

It is probable that the little prince first saw
the light in the royal palace at Thebes, which
was situated on the edge of the desert at the
foot of the western hills. It was, as has been
said, an extensive building, lightly constructed
and gaily decorated. The ceilings and pave-
ments of its halls were fantastically painted
with scenes of animal life: wild cattle ran

through reedy swamps beneath the royal feet, and there many-coloured fish swam in the water; while overhead flights of pigeons, white against a blue sky, passed across the hall, and wild duck hastened towards the open casements. Through curtained doorways one might obtain glimpses of the garden planted with flowers foreign to Egypt; and on the east of the palace shone the great pleasure-lake, surrounded by the trees of Asia.

In all the world there are few places more beautiful than the site of this palace. Here one may sit for many an hour watching the changing colours on the wonderful cliffs, the pink and the yellow of the rocks standing out from the blue and the purple of the deep shadows. In the fields which now surround the ruined palace, where the royal gardens were laid out, one obtains an impression of colour, of beauty, and of gaiety —if it can be so expressed—which is not easily equalled. The continuous sunshine and the bracing wind render one intensely awake to natural joys; and here, indeed, was a fitting birthplace, one feels, for a king who taught his people to study the beauties of nature.

2. THE RISE OF ATON.

The little prince was named Amonhotep,[1] "the Peace-of-Amon," after his father; but though the supremacy of Amon was thus acknowledged, the Heliopolitan deity appears to have been considered as the protector of the young boy. While the luxurious court rejoiced at the birth of their future king, one feels that the ancient priesthood of Amon-Ra must have looked askance at the baby who was destined one day to be their master. This priesthood still demanded implicit obedience to its stiff and ancient conventions, and it refused to recognise the growing tendency towards religious speculation.

Probably stronger measures would have been taken by it to resist the growing power of Ra-Horakhti, had it not been for the fact that Ra was also a form of Amon, and had been identified with him under the name of Amon-Ra. The god Amon was originally but the local deity of

---

[1] He took the name Akhnaton in about the sixth year of his reign.

Thebes; and, when the Theban Pharaohs of the Eighteenth Dynasty had elevated him to the position of the state god of all Egypt, they made him acceptable to the various provinces, as we have seen, by pointing to his identification with Ra, the sun-god, who, under one form or another, found a place in every temple and held high rank in every variety of mythology. As Amon-Ra he was able to be appreciated by the sun-worshippers of Syria and by those of Nubia, for there were few races who would not do homage to the great giver of warmth and light.

It is possible that those more thoughtful members of the court who were quietly attempting to undermine the influence of the priesthood of Amon, and who were beginning to carry into execution the schemes of emancipation which we have already noticed, now endeavoured to strip Amon of his association with the sun; for that identity was really his simple claim to acceptance by any but Thebans. The priesthood, on their part, it may be supposed, drew as much attention as possible to the connection of their deity with Ra; for they knew that none but the Heliopolitan god could be advanced with success as a rival of Amon by those who desired to overthrow the Theban god. Thus one finds that the High Priest of Ra at Heliopolis was given, and was obliged to accept, the honorary office of Second Priest of Amon at Thebes,[1] which at once placed him under the thumb of the Theban High Priest. The propounders of the new thought, however, met this move by bringing into greater prominence the claims, not of Ra - Horakhti, but of Aton, which was merely a more elusive form of the sun - god. The priesthood of Amon had always checked the individual growth of Ra-Horakhti by regarding him simply as an aspect of Ra, and hence of Amon - Ra. One of the essential features of the new movement was the regarding of Ra as an aspect of Ra-Horakhti, and the calling of Ra-Horakhti by the uncontaminated name of Aton. Aton, in fact, was originally introduced into the matter largely for the purpose of preventing any identification between Amon-Ra and Ra-Horakhti. Soon the name of Aton, entirely supplanting that of Atum, was heard with some frequency at Thebes and

[1] His statue is at Turin. See also Erman, 'Life in Ancient Egypt,' p. 297.

elsewhere, but always, it must be remembered, as another word for Ra-Horakhti.

The desire of the court for a change of religion is understandable. The cult of the god Amon, as has been said, was so hedged about with conventionalities that free thought was impossible. We have seen, however, that the upper classes were passing through a phase of religious speculation, and they were ready to revolt against the domination of a priesthood which forbade criticism. The worship of the intangible power of the sun, under the name of Aton, offered endless possibilities for the exercise of those tendencies towards the abstract which were now beginning to be felt all over the civilised world. This was man's first age of philosophical thought, and for the first time in history the gods were being endued with ideal qualities.

Apart from all questions of religion, the priesthood of Amon had obtained such power and wealth that it was a very serious menace to the dignity of the throne. The great organisation which had its headquarters at Karnak had become an incubus which weighed heavily upon the state. For political reasons alone, therefore, it was desirable to push the priests of Heliopolis into a more prominent position.

There was, moreover, a third consideration. The god Aton, with whom Ra and Ra-Horakhti were now being identified, was, we have seen, originally the same as the Syrian and Greek Adonis, the word " Adon " or " Aton " meaning simply "lord." Thus the propounders of the new doctrines must have dreamt of an Egypto-Syrian empire bound together by the ties of a common religion. With one god understood and worshipped from the cataracts of the Nile to the distant Euphrates, what power could destroy the empire ?

3. THE POWER OF QUEEN TIY.

In Amonhotep III. one may see the lazy, speculative Oriental, too opinionated and too vain to bear with the stiff routine of his fathers, and yet too lacking in energy to formulate a new religion. On the other hand, there is every reason to suppose that Queen

Tiy possessed the ability to impress the claims
of the new thought upon her husband's mind,
and gradually to turn his eyes, and those of
the court, away from the sombre worship of
Amon, "the unknown god," into the direction
of the brilliant cult of the sun. Those who
have travelled in Egypt will realise how completely the land is dominated by the sun.
The blue skies, the shining rocks, the golden
desert, the verdant fields, all seem to cry out
for joy of the sunshine. The extraordinary
energy which one may feel in Egypt at
sunrise, and the deep melancholy which sometimes accompanies the red nightfall, must have
been felt by Tiy also in her palace at Thebes.

As the years passed the power and influence
of Queen Tiy increased; and now that she
had borne a son to the king there was added
to her great position as royal wife the equally
great *rôle* of royal mother. Never before
had a queen been so freely represented on
all the king's monuments, nor had so fine a
series of titles been given before to the wife
of a Pharaoh. At Sedênga, far up in the
Sudan, her husband erected a temple for her;

and in distant Sinai a beautiful portrait head
of her was recently found. All visitors to
Thebes have seen her figures by the side of
the legs of the two great colossi at the edge
of the Western Desert ; and the huge statues
of herself and, her husband, now in the Cairo
Museum, will have been seen by those who
have visited that collection. Of Gilukhipa,[1]
however, and the king's other wives, one hears
nothing at all : Queen Tiy relegated them to
the background almost before their marriage
ceremonies were over.

By the time that Amonhotep III. had reigned
for thirty years or so, he had ceased to give
much attention to state affairs, and the power
had almost entirely passed into the capable
hands of Tiy. Already an influence, which we
may presume to have been to a large extent
hers, was being felt in many directions : Ra-
Horakhti and Aton were being brought into
the foreground, a tone of thought which can
hardly be regarded as purely Egyptian was
being developed, the art was undergoing modi-
fications and had risen to a pitch of excellence

[1] Page 39.

never attained before or after. The exquisite low-reliefs of the end of the reign of Amonhotep III.—for example, those to be seen at Thebes in the tombs of Khaemhat and Rames,[1] both of which are definitely dated to the close of the reign—stir one almost as do the works of the early Florentine masters. There is an elusive grace in the dainty figures there sculptured, which, through another medium and under other laws of convention, cause them to appeal with the same force of indefinable sweetness as do the figures in the works of Filipino Lippi and Botticelli. In the mass of Egyptian painting and sculpture of secondary importance such gems as these have been overlooked and have not been appreciated by the public; but the present writer ventures to think that some day they will set the heart of all art-lovers dancing as danced those of Queen Tiy's great masters.

The court in which the little prince passed his earliest years was more brilliant than ever it had been before, and Queen Tiy presided over scenes of indescribable splendour. Amonhotep

---

[1] Recently discovered by the present writer whilst repairing this tomb.

III. has been truly called "the Magnificent";
and at no period, save that of Thothmes III.,
were the royal treasuries so full or the nobles so
wealthy. Out of a pageant of festivities, from
amidst the noise of song and laughter, the little
sad-eyed prince first emerges on to the stage
of history, led by the hand of Queen Tiy; but
as he appears before us, above the clink of the
golden wine - bowls, above the sound of the
timbrels, one seems to hear the lilt of a more
simple song, and the peaceful singing of a lark.

4. AKHNATON'S MARRIAGE.

During the last years of his reign the Pharaoh,
although well under fifty years of age,[1] seems to
have suffered from permanent ill - health. On
two occasions the King of Mitanni sent to
Egypt a miracle-working statuette of the goddess Ishtar, apparently in the hope that Amonhotep might be cured of his illness by it. It
is probable that the king had never been a very
strong man. Having been born when his father

---

[1] His mummy is that of a man of not more than fifty.

—himself extremely delicate—was but a child, he had had little chance of enjoying a robust middle age, and he passed on to his children this inherent weakness.   One hears no more of his daughters,[1] whom we have seen mourning for their grandparents Yuaa and Tuau, and there is some likelihood that they died young. The little Prince Amonhotep was already developing constitutional weaknesses which rendered his life very precarious.   His skull was misshapen, and he must have been subject to occasional epileptic fits.   And now Queen Tiy gave birth to a daughter, who was named Baketaton in honour of the new god, and who seems to have lived less than a score of years, since nothing more is heard of her after her twelfth or thirteenth year.

As Amonhotep, at the age of forty-eight or forty-nine, felt his end approaching, he seems to have shown considerable anxiety in regard to the succession.   Here was his only son—now a boy of ten or eleven years of age—in so sad a state of health that he could not be expected

---

[1] The wise man Amonhotep-son-of-Hapu was steward of Princess Setamon's estate, but this may have been previous to her mention in her grandparents' tomb.

Amonhotep III.

to live to manhood, and in the event of his
death the throne would be without an occupant
in the direct line. Obviously it was necessary
that he should be married as soon as possible, in
order that he might become a father as early
as that was naturally possible. Amonhotep III.
himself had been married to Tiy when he was
about twelve years of age, and his father Thothmes IV. had likewise been married at that
early age.[1] The little Prince Amonhotep should,
therefore, also be given a wife at once; and the
Pharaoh now began to look around for a suit-
able consort for him. He had heard that
Dushratta, King of Mitanni, had a small
daughter who was said to be a comely maiden;
but it appears that she was only eight or nine
years of age,[2] and therefore could not be expected to provide an heir for at least another
four years. Nevertheless there were many political reasons for proposing the union. Mitanni
was, as we have seen, the buffer state between
the Pharaoh's Syrian possessions and the lands of
the Hittites and of the Mesopotamians. Thothmes
IV. had asked a bride from Mitanni, and Amonhotep III. himself had obtained Gilukhipa from

[1] Page 111.   [2] Page 56.

thence, if not Queen Tiy also : both these being probably political matches, designed for the welfare of the Syrian empire. The Pharaoh therefore decided upon this marriage for his sickly son, and sent an embassy to Dushratta to negotiate the union between these two children.

The reply of Dushratta has, fortunately, been preserved to us. The Mitannian king acknowledges the arrival of the envoy, and is much rejoiced at this further binding together of the two countries. In a subsequent letter it is evident that the princess has already been sent to Egypt, and we are led to suppose that Prince Amonhotep has at once been married to her. The little princess was named Tadukhipa, but on her arrival in Egypt she was renamed Nefertiti. Her age, as mentioned above, is apparent from the fact that, although in after life she gave birth to children at very regular intervals, her first child was not born until nearly five years after her marriage.[1] So young was

[1] It is usual for Egyptian girls to become mothers at about the age of thirteen, though sometimes earlier. They often continue to bear children at intervals of about two years, over a period of thirty years or so. Fifteen children is thus the usual number of a family, but half these generally die in babyhood.

she that she did not at once cohabit with the prince, but was put under the care of a certain lady of the court named Ty, the wife of a noble of the name of Ay, who afterwards usurped the throne. This lady Ty called herself in later years "great nurse and nourisher of the Queen," and Ay always called himself the king's father-in-law (*neter at*). It would thus seem that they had become the actual foster-parents of the little Syrian girl. It was not at all unusual in Egypt for a child to be adopted thus; and it is a curious fact that if a woman gave the breast to a child of any age but for a moment, or if a man placed his finger in the child's mouth, a formal adoption was considered to have been made.[1]

The court had hardly settled down after the celebration of the marriage of Amonhotep and Tadukhipa - Nefertiti, when it was thrown into mourning by the death of Amonhotep "the Magnificent," which occurred in the thirty-sixth year of his reign. Queen Tiy at once assumed control of state affairs, on behalf of her barely eleven-year-old son, who as Amonhotep IV. now ascended the throne of the Pharaohs.

[1] Maspero.

5. THE ACCESSION OF AKHNATON.

On coming to the throne the young king
fixed his titulary in the following manner :—

> Mighty Bull, Lofty of Plumes; Favourite of the
> Two Goddesses, Great in Kingship in Karnak;
> Golden Hawk, Wearer of Diadems in the Southern
> Heliopolis; King of Upper and Lower Egypt,
> Beautiful-is-the-Being-of-Ra, the Only-One-of-
> Ra; Son of the Sun, Peace-of-Amon (Amonhotep),
> Divine Ruler of Thebes; Great in Duration, Living
> for Ever and Ever, Beloved of Amon-Ra, Lord of
> Heaven.

These titles were drawn up on more or less
prescribed lines, and conformed to the old custom
of the Pharaohs. Like his ancestors, he was
called "Beloved of Amon-Ra," although, as we
have seen, the power of that god was already
much undermined. To counterbalance this reference to the god of Thebes, however, one finds
the surprising title—

> High Priest of Ra-Horakhti, rejoicing in the horizon
> in his name, "Heat-which-is-in-Aton."

Let the boy be said to be beloved of Amon-Ra
till the walls of Thebes reverberate with the cry;

Akhnaton.

let Amon-Ra be called Lord of Heaven till the
priestly heralds can shout no more : the doom of
the god of Thebes cannot now be averted, for the
reigning Pharaoh is dedicated to another god.

It is obvious that a boy of eleven years of age
could not himself have claimed the office of the
High Priest of Ra - Horakhti. Queen Tiy and
her advisers must have deliberately endowed the
youthful king with this office, largely in order
to set the seal upon the fate of Amon. There
were, perhaps, other reasons why this remarkable
step was decided upon. It may be, as has been
said, that the queen, before the birth of her
son, had vowed him to Ra-Horakhti. Again, the
boy was epileptic, was subject to hallucinations;
and it may be that while in this condition he
had seen visions or uttered words which led his
mother to believe him to be the chosen one of the
Heliopolitan god, whose name the prince must
have been constantly hearing. In a palace where
the mystical " Heat-which-is-in-Aton," which was
the new elaboration of the god's name, was
being daily invoked, and where the youthful
master of Egypt was constantly falling into
what appeared to be holy frenzy, it is not

unlikely that the rising deity would be connected with the eccentricities of the young
Pharaoh. The High Priest of Ra-Horakhti was
always called "The Great of Visions," and was
thus essentially a visionary prophet either by
nature or by circumstance; and the unfortunate
boy's physical condition may have been turned,
thus, to account in the struggle against Amon-Ra.

One may now imagine the Pharaoh as a pale,
sickly youth. His head seemed too large for
his body; his eyelids were heavy; his eyes as
one imagines them were wells of dream. His
features were delicately moulded, and his mouth,
in spite of a somewhat protruding lower jaw,
is reminiscent of the best of the art of Rossetti.
He seems to have been a quiet, studious boy,
whose thoughts wandered in fair places, searching for that happiness which his physical condition had denied to him. His nature was
gentle; his young heart overflowed with love.
He delighted, it would seem, to walk in the
gardens of the palace, to hear the birds singing,
to watch the fish in the lake, to smell the
flowers, to follow the butterflies, to warm his
small bones in the sunshine. There was a grave

dignity in his gait, or the artists have lied; and his words were already fraught with wisdom. The great crown of the Pharaohs sat easily upon his head, for his every movement was royal. He accepted as his due the homage of the court; yet he does not seem to have acted with arrogance, and was ever a tender-hearted, impulsive child. Already he was sometimes called "Lord of the Breath of Sweetness"; [1] and already he was so much beloved by his subjects that their adherence to him through the rough places of his future life was assured. For the first years of his reign he was, of course, entirely under the regency of his mother. Dushratta, the King of Mitanni, writing to congratulate the boy on his accession, addressed himself to Queen Tiy, as though he thought the king would hardly yet be able to understand a letter; and in a later communication he asks the Pharaoh to inquire of his mother as to certain matters of international policy. But although so young, the king was wise beyond his years, as the reader will presently see.

---

[1] Scarabs of the early period are sometimes inscribed *Neb-nef-nezem*, which has this meaning.

6. THE FIRST YEARS OF AKHNATON'S REIGN.

In a subsequent chapter it will be the writer's purpose to show to what heights of ideal thought, and to what profundities of religious and moral philosophy, this boy, in the years of his early manhood, attained; and it will but enhance our respect for his abilities when he reached maturity, if we find in his early training all manner of shortcomings. The beautiful doctrines of the religion with which this Pharaoh's name is identified were productions of his later days; and until he was at least seventeen years of age neither his exalted monotheism nor any of his future principles were really apparent. Some time after the eighth year of his reign one finds that he had evolved a religion so pure that one must compare it with Christianity in order to discover its faults; and the reader will presently see that this superb theology was not derived from his education.

One of the first acts of the king's reign, undertaken at the desire of Queen Tiy or of the royal advisers, was the erection of a temple to Ra-

Horakhti Aton at Karnak.[1] This was in no way an insult to Amon, for Thothmes III. and other Pharaohs had dedicated temples at Karnak to gods other than Amon. The priesthood of Amon-Ra recognised the existence of the many deities of Egypt, and gave them their place in the constitution of heaven, reserving for their own god the title of "King of the Gods." There was a temple of Ptah here; there were shrines set apart for the worship of Min; and other gods, unconnected with Amon, were here accommodated. The priests of Amon-Ra thus could not offer any serious objection to the project. The building [2] was to be constructed of sandstone, and therefore various officials were dispatched to the great quarries of Gebel Silsileh, which lie on the river between Edfu and Kom Ombo, and to those near Esneh. Large tablets were there carved upon the cliffs towards the close of the work, and on them the figure of the

[1] The date of this work is not exactly known, but as it was certainly finished before the king founded his new city, it must have been commenced immediately upon his accession.

[2] The word benben, "shrine," has the hieroglyph of an obelisk at the end of it, which has led to some mistranslations. Perhaps the temple was built somewhat on the plan of that at Abusêr, where an obelisk stood in an open court.

Pharaoh was represented worshipping Amon, who was thus still the state god. Above the king's figure, however, the disk of the sun is seen, and from it a number of lines, representing rays, project downwards towards the royal figure. These rays terminate in hands, which thus seem to be distributing the "heat-which-is-in-Aton" around the Pharaoh. This is the first representation of the afterwards famous symbol of the religion of Aton, and it is significant that it should make its *début* in a scene representing the worship of Amon.

The king is called the High Priest of Ra-Horakhti; but the title "Living in truth," which he took to himself in later years, and which had reference to the religion of Aton which he was soon to evolve, does not yet appear.

A large number of fragments from this shrine have been discovered, and on these one sees references to the gods Horus, Set, Wepwat, and others. The king is still called by the name Amonhotep, which was later banned, and the names of Aton, afterwards always written within the royal ovals or cartouches, are still lacking in that distinction. The temple was called "Aton-is-found-in-the-House-of-Aton," a curious name of which the meaning is not clear.[1] A certain official named Hataay was "Scribe and Overseer of the Granary of the House of the Aton," by which this temple is probably meant; and in the tomb of Rames a reference is made to the building by its full name, and a picture of it is given, but otherwise one knows little about it. The rapidity with which it was desired to be set up is shown by the fact that the great, well-trimmed blocks of stone usually employed in the construction of sacred buildings were largely dispensed with, and only small easily-handled blocks were used. The imperfections in the building were then hidden by a judicious use of plaster and cement, and thus the walls were smoothed for the reception of the reliefs. The quarter in which the temple stood was now called "Brightness of Aton the Great," and Thebes received the new name of "City of the Brightness of Aton."

There are two other monuments which date from these early years of the king's reign : both are tombs of great nobles. At this period one of the greatest personages in the land was the

[1] It is possible that "found" is a mistranslation.

above-mentioned Rames, the Vizir of Upper Egypt. This official was now engaged in constructing and decorating a magnificent sepulchre for himself in the Theban necropolis. In the great hall of this tomb the artists were busy preparing the beautiful sculptures and paintings which were to cover the walls, and ere half their work was finished they set themselves to the making of a fine figure of Amonhotep IV. seated upon his throne, with the goddess Maat standing behind him. The scene was probably executed a few months before the making of the tablets at the quarries. The sun's rays do not appear, and the work was carried out strictly according to the canons of art obtaining during the last years of Amonhotep III. and the first of his son. But hardly had the figures been finished before the order came that the Aton rays had to be included, and certain changes in the art had to be recognised; and therefore the artists set to work upon another figure of the king standing under these many-handed beams of "heat," and now accompanied by his, as yet, childless wife. The two scenes may be seen by visitors to Thebes standing side by side, and

nowhere may the contrast between the old order
of things and the new be so clearly observed.

While Rames was providing a tomb for
himself at Thebes, another great noble named
Horemheb, who ultimately usurped the throne,
was constructing his sepulchre at Sakkârah,
the Memphite necropolis near Cairo. Horemheb was commander-in-chief of the army, and
in his tomb some superb reliefs are carved
showing him receiving rewards in that capacity
from the king. Some of the scenes represent
the arrival of Asiatic refugees in Egypt, who
ask to be allowed to take up their abode on
the banks of the Nile, and the figures of these
foreigners rank amongst the finest specimens of
Egyptian art. In the inscriptions, Horemheb,
who is supposed to be addressing the king,
states that the Pharaoh owes his throne to
Amon,[1] but yet we see that the figure of the
king is drawn in that style of art which is
typical of the new religion.[2]

---

[1] Thus corresponding to the Silsileh quarry tablet, where Amon
is worshipped.

[2] This tomb of Horemheb seems to have been begun and finished
in the early years of Akhnaton's reign, to have been left alone during the remainder of the reign, and to have received the addition

7. THE NEW ART.

This sudden change in the style of the reliefs which we have observed in these two tombs and on the quarry tablets seems to be attributable to about the fourth year of the king's reign. The reliefs which were now carved upon the walls of the new temple of Ra-Horakhti at Karnak show us a style of art quite different from that of the king's early years. The figure of the Pharaoh, which the artists in the tomb of Rames represented as standing below the newly - invented sun's rays, is as different from the earlier figure there executed as chalk is from cheese. The Pharaoh whom we see in the tomb of Horemheb and on the quarry tablets is represented, according to canons of art, entirely different from those existing at the king's accession.

of doorposts (see note on p. 265) after the death of Akhnaton. Fragments of the tomb are now divided between Leiden, Bologna, Vienna, Alexandria, and Cairo; and it would seem that all except those in the Cairo museum (the doorposts) are from the earlier period. The titles on the Cairo fragments are far more elaborate than those on the others. See Breasted, Records, iii. 1 ff.

In the drawing of the human figure, and especially that of the Pharaoh, there are three very distinct characteristics in this new style of art. Firstly, as to the head: the skull is elongated; the chin, as seen in profile, is drawn as though it were sharply pointed; the flesh under the jaw is skimped, thus giving an upward turn to the line; and the neck is represented as being long and thin. Secondly, the stomach is made to obtrude itself upon the attention by being drawn as though from a fat and ungainly model. And thirdly, the hips and thighs are abnormally large, though from the knee downwards the legs are of more natural size. This distortion of human anatomy is marked in a lesser degree in all the lines of the body; and the whole figure becomes a startling type of an art which seems at first to have sprung fully developed from the brain of the boy-Pharaoh or from one of the eccentrics of the court.

The king was now fifteen years old, and seems to have been extraordinarily mature for his age. It may be that he had objected to be represented in the conventional manner, and had told his artists to draw him as he was. The elongated skull, the pointed chin, and even, perhaps, the protruding paunch, may thus have originated. But the ungainly thighs could only be accounted for by some radical deformity in the royal model, and that he was a well-made man in this respect his recently discovered bones most clearly show.

Purely tentatively a suggestion may here be offered to account for this peculiar treatment of the human body. It is probable that the king had now, in a boyish way, become deeply interested in the religious contest which was beginning to be waged between Amon - Ra and Ra - Horakhti Aton. Having listened to the arguments on both sides, it may have occurred to him to study for himself the ancient documents and inscriptions bearing on the matter. In so doing, he would have found that Amon had become the state god only some few hundred years before his own time, and that previous to his ascent to this important position, previous even to the earliest mention of his name, Ra-Horakhti had been supreme. Carrying his inquiries back, past the days of the pyramid

kings to the archaic Pharaohs who reigned at
the dim beginning of things, he would still have
found the Heliopolitan god worshipped. One
of the Pharaohs' most cherished titles was "Son
of the Sun," which, as we have seen, had been
borne by each successive sovereign since the
days of the Fifth Dynasty, whose kings claimed
descent from Ra himself. Such studies would
inevitably bring two matters into prominence :
firstly, that Amon was, after all, but a usurper ;
and, secondly, that as Pharaoh he was the
descendant of Ra - Horakhti, and was that god's
representative on earth.

On these grounds, more than on any others,
all things connected with Amon would become
distasteful to him. He was too young to understand fully which of the two religions was the
better morally or theologically ; but he was
old enough to be moved by the romance of
history, and to feel that those great, shadowy
Pharaohs who lived when the world was young,
and who at the dawn of events worshipped the
sun, were the truest and best examples for him
to follow. They were his ancestors, and as they
were the sons of Ra, so he, too, was the proud

descendant of that great god. In his veins
there ran the blood of the sun, that "heat-
which-is-in-Aton" pulsed through and through
him; and the more he read in those old documents the more he was stirred by the glory
of that distant past when men worshipped the
god whose rights Amon had usurped. Now the
canons of art were regarded as a distinctly
religious institution, and the methods of treating
the human figure then in vogue had in the first
place the sanction of the priesthood of Amon;
and few things would be more upsetting to
their *régime* than the abandoning of these canons.
This was probably recognised by those who
were furthering the cause of Ra - Horakhti, and
the young king may have been assisted and
encouraged in his views. Presently it may
have been brought home to him that, since he
was thus the representative of those archaic
kings and the High Priest of their god, it was
fitting that the canons acknowledged by those
far - off ancestors should be recognised by him.
Here, then, he would both please his own
romantic fancy and deal a blow at the Amon
priesthood by banning the art which they upheld,

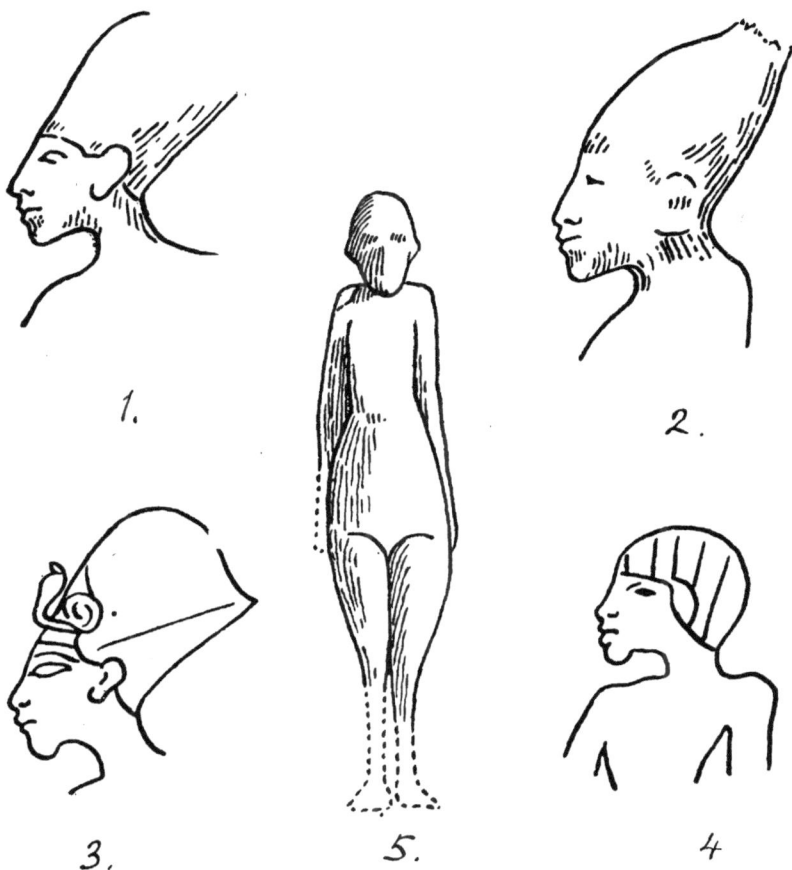

The Art of Akhnaton compared with Archaic Art.

1. The head of Akhnaton.   From a contemporary drawing.
2. The head of a king.   From an archaic statuette found by Professor Petrie at Abydos.
3. The head of Akhnaton.   From a contemporary drawing.
4. The head of a prince.   From an archaic tablet found by Professor Petrie at Abydos.
5. An archaic statuette found by Professor Petrie at Diospolis, showing the large thighs
    found in the art of Akhnaton.

and by infusing into the sculptures and paintings of his time something of the spirit of the most ancient art of Egypt.

In the old temples of Heliopolis and elsewhere a few relics of that period, no doubt, were still preserved; and the king was thus able to study the wood and slate carvings and the ivory figures of archaic times. We of the present day can also study such figures, a few specimens having been brought to light by modern excavators; and the similarity between the treatment of the human body in this archaic art and the new art of Akhnaton at once becomes apparent. In the accompanying illustrations some archaic figures are shown, and one may perhaps see in them the origin of the idiosyncrasies of the new school. Here and in all representations of archaic men one sees the elongated skull so characteristic of the king's style; in the ivory figure of an archaic Pharaoh one sees the well-known droop of Akhnaton's head and his pointed chin; in the clay and ivory figures is the prominent stomach; and here also, most apparent of all, are the unaccountably large thighs and ponderous hips.

Akhnaton's art might thus be said to be a kind of renaissance—a return to the classical period of archaic days; the underlying motive of this return being the desire to lay emphasis upon the king's character as the representative of that most ancient of all gods, Ra-Horakhti.

Another feature of the new religion now becomes apparent. In the worship of Ra-Horakhti Aton there was an endeavour to do honour to the Pharaoh as the son of the sun, and to the god as the founder of the royal line. Tradition stated that Ra or Ra-Horakhti had once reigned upon earth, and that his spirit had passed from Pharaoh to Pharaoh. This god was thus the only true King of Heaven, and Amon was but a usurper of much more recent date. It was for this reason that the names of the new god were placed within royal cartouches; and for this reason the king was so careful to call Ra-Horakhti his "father," and to name him "god and king." For this reason also Akhnaton often wore the crown of Lower Egypt which was

used at Heliopolis, but never the crown of
Upper Egypt, which history told him did not
exist when Ra ruled on earth.[1]

Apart from the representation of the human
form, the new art is chiefly characterised by
its freedom of poses. An attempt is made to
break away from tradition, and a desire is
shown to have done with the conventions of
the age. Never before had the artists caught
the swing of a walk, the relaxation of a
seated figure, so well or so truthfully. Sculpture in the round now reached a height of
perfection which places it above all but the
art of the Greeks in the old world; and
there is a grace and naturalness in the low-
reliefs which command one's admiration.

There are only two artists of the period
who are known by name. The one was a
certain ·Auta, who is represented in a relief
dating from some eight years after the change
in the art had taken place. It is a significant
fact that this personage held the post of master-

---

[1] We know from the "Palermo stone" that the kingdom of
Lower Egypt was much more ancient than that of Upper Egypt.

artist to Queen Tiy; and it is possible that in him and his patron we have the originators of the movement. The king, however, was now old enough to take an active interest in such matters; and the other artist who is known by name, a certain Bek, definitely states that the king himself taught him. Thus there is reason to suppose that the young Pharaoh's own hand is to be traced in the new canons, although they were instituted when he was but fifteen years old.

8. THE NEW RELIGION DEVELOPS.

There is an interesting record, apparently dating from about this period, which is to be seen upon the rocks near the breccia quarries of Wady Hammamât. Here there are three cartouches standing upon two *neb* signs, symbolic of sovereignty, and above them is the disk and rays of the new religion. One of these cartouches, surmounted by the tall feathers worn by the queens of this period, contains a very short name, which can only be that of Queen

The Artist Auta.

Tiy.[1] The other two cartouches contain the names Amonhotep (IV.) and the Pharaoh's second designation. Thus we see that after the new religious symbol had been introduced, and just before the king took the name of "Akhnaton," Queen Tiy still held equal royal rank with him, and was evidently Regent.

During the fifteenth to the seventeenth years of his age the king devoted a considerable amount of time and thought to the changes which were taking place. With the enthusiasm of youth he threw himself into the new movement, and one may suppose that it required all Queen Tiy's tact and diplomacy to keep him from offending his country by some rash action against the priesthood of Amon. Those priests were by no means reconciled to the king's devotion to Ra-Horakhti; and although he still nominally served the Theban god, they felt that every day he was becoming more estranged from that deity. No doubt there were many pass-

[1] In later times the name of Tiy and the Pharaoh's second name were erased, but the name Amonhotep was not damaged. The facsimile copy here given was made on the spot by the present writer in correction of a previous copy made by Golénischeff. It is published in his 'Travels in the Upper Egyptian Deserts' (Blackwood).

ages of arms between the High Priest of Amon-Ra and this royal High Priest of the sun, young as he was. The new art, upsetting all the old religious conventions, was distasteful to the priests; the new religious thought did not conform to their stereotyped doctrines; and much that the king said was absolutely heretical to their ears. The tide of new thought, directed in so eager and boyishly unreserved a manner, was sweeping them from their feet, and they knew not whither they were being carried.

The court officials blindly followed their young king, and to every word which he spoke they listened attentively. Sometimes the thoughts which he voiced came direct from the mazes of his own mind; sometimes perhaps he repeated the utterances of his deep-thinking mother; and sometimes there passed from his lips the pearls of wisdom which he had gleaned from the wise men of his court. It had been the boy's desire to listen to the dreams of the East, to receive into his brain those speculations which ever meander so charmedly through the lands more near the sunrise. At his behest the dreamers of Asia related to him their visions;

the philosophers made pregnant his mind with
the mystery of knowledge; the poets sung to
him harp-songs in which echoed the cry of the
elder days; the priests of strange gods sub-
mitted to him the creeds of strange people.
To him was made known the sweetness of the
legends of Greece. The laughter of the woods
rang in his ears, though never in narrow
Egypt had he felt the enchantment of great
forests. He had not seen the mountains, and
the wooded slopes which rise from the Mediterranean were scenes but dreamed of; and yet
it was the flute of Pan and the song of the
nymphs in the mountain streams which set the
thoughts dancing within his misshapen skull.
He had not walked in the shadow of the cedars
of Lebanon, nor had he ascended the Syrian
hills; but nevertheless the hymns of Adonis and
the chants of Baal were as familiar to him as
were the solemn chants of Amon-Ra. The rose-
gardens of Persia, the incense-groves of Araby,
added their philosophies to his dreams, and the
haunting lips of Babylon whispered to him
tales of far-off days. From Sardinia, Sicily,
Crete, and Cyprus there came to him the

doctrines of those who had business in great waters; and Libya and Ethiopia disclosed their mysteries to his eager ears. The fertile brain of the Pharaoh was thus sown at an early age with the seed of all that was wonderful in the world of thought.

It must always be remembered that the king had much foreign blood in his veins. On the other hand, those men to whom he spoke, though highly educated, were but superstitious Egyptians who could not relieve themselves of the belief that a divine power rested upon the Pharaoh. Thus his speculative young brain poured its fantasies into attentive minds unbiassed by rival speculations, though narrowed by conventions. Egyptians, ever lacking in originality, have always possessed the power to imitate and adapt; and those nobles whose fortunes were dependent upon the royal favour soon learnt to attune their minds to the note of their king. Daily they must have gone about their business ostentatiously attempting to hold to the difficult path of truth; laboriously telling themselves what wonders the new thought revealed to them; loudly praising the wisdom of the boy-Pharaoh;

and nervously asking themselves whether and when the wrath of Amon would smite them.

Thus encouraged, the king and his mother developed their speculations, and drew into their circle of followers some of the greatest nobles of the land. A striking example of this proselytising is to be found in the tomb of the Vizir Rames. It has already been stated that that official had constructed for himself a sepulchre in the Theban necropolis, upon the walls of which he had first caused a portrait of the young king to be sculptured in the old conventional style, and later had added another portrait of the Pharaoh standing beneath the radiating beams of the sun, executed in the new style. Rames now added various other scenes and inscriptions, and he records a certain speech made by the king to him, and his own reply.

"The words of Ra," the king had said, "are before thee. . . . My august father [1] taught me their essence and [revealed] them to me. . . . They were known in my heart, opened to my face. I understood. . . ."

"Thou art the Only One of Aton; in possession

---

[1] Meaning the god.

F

of his designs," replied Rames. "Thou hast directed the mountains. The fear of thee is in the midst of their secret chambers, as it is in the hearts of the people. The mountains hearken to thee as the people hearken."

Thus one sees how the king was already formulating some kind of doctrine in his head, and that the nobles were receiving it; but it is significant that there are here representations of Rames loaded with gifts by the Pharaoh, as though in reward for his allegiance. The Pharaoh seems, indeed, to have showered honours upon those who appeared to grasp intelligently the thoughts which were still immature in his own head; and there must have been many an antagonist who rallied to his standard from the sheer love of gold. The king was in need of all the support which he could muster, for an open break with the priesthood of Amon-Ra grew more and more probable as his doctrines shaped themselves in his mind; and although the people of Egypt as a whole would, without question, follow their Pharaoh for the one reason that he *was* Pharaoh, there was every probability that the Amon priesthood and the Theban populace would make something of a stand against any infringement of the rights of their local god.

The young Pharaoh seems to have been very popular, and one may presume that he inherited, from his illustrious fathers, the charm of manner which there is not a little evidence to show they possessed. Throughout his life, and for some years after his death, he retained the affection of his people; and when one considers how faithfully his nobles followed him so long as he had strength and health to lead them, and how completely lost they were at his death, one realises how great an influence he must have exerted over them. Even at this early age they seem to have possessed a deep regard for the grave, thoughtful boy; and behind all the pretence, the hypocrisy, and the merely conventional loyalty, one surely catches a glimpse of a strong, personal affection for the king.

We must here record the birth of the king's first daughter, which occurred in about the fifth year of his reign, when he was some sixteen years of age, and when Nefertiti was about thirteen years old. The child was named Merytaton, "Beloved of Aton"; and though the advent of

a daughter instead of a son must have been a
grave disappointment to the royal couple, a remarkable degree of affection was lavished upon
the little girl, as will be apparent in the sequel.

9. THE NATURE OF THE NEW RELIGION.

There was nothing strikingly exalted in the
religion which was now so filling the king's mind.
Ra-Horakhti Aton was in no wise considered as
the only god : there were as yet no ideas of
monotheism in the doctrine. In the new temple
at Karnak, as we have seen, Horus, Set, Wepwat,
and other gods were named ; and elsewhere
Amon was reluctantly recognised. The goddess
Maat, in the tomb of Rames, was not obliterated
from the walls, but still stood protecting the king ;
and in the same tomb Horus of Edfu is invoked.
In the tomb of Horemheb, Horus, Osiris, Isis,
Nephthys, and Hathor are mentioned, and the
gods of the Necropolis still receive honour ;
Horemheb himself still holds the honorary post
of High Priest of Horus, Lord of Alabastronpolis ;
Thoth and Maat are referred to ; and there is

a magical prayer to Ra, which is by no means of lofty character. Scarabs of this period, speak of the Pharaoh as beloved of Thoth. And in a letter to the king dated in the fifth year of his reign, Ptah and "the gods and goddesses" of Memphis are referred to.

This letter is of such interest that a fuller account of it must here be given. It was addressed to the king, who is still called Amon-hotep, by a royal steward named Apiy, who lived at Memphis. Two copies of the letter were found at, Gurob,[1] both dated in the fifth year of the king's reign, the third month of winter, and the nineteenth day. The letter begins with the full titles of the Pharaoh, including the phrase "living in truth," which from this time onwards was always added to his name. Then follows the invocation: "May Ptah of the beautiful countenance work for thee, who created thy beauties, thy true father who raised (?) thee from his house to rule the orbit of the Aton." Next comes the real business of the letter: "A communication is this to the Master, [to whom be] life, prosperity, and

---

[1] Griffith: Kahun Papyri. Text, p. 91.

health, to give information that the temple of
thy father Ptah . . . is sound and prosperous;
the house of Pharaoh . . . is flourishing; the
establishments of Pharaoh . . . are flourishing;
the residence of Pharaoh . . . is flourishing and
healthy; the offerings of all the gods and goddesses who are upon the soil (?) of Memphis are
. . . complete; complete [are they] there is nothing
delayed from them." Again the titles of the king
are given, and the letter ends with the date.

Thus in the fifth year of the king's reign,
when he was about sixteen years of age, the
various gods of Egypt were still acknowledged;
and, though the art had been changed and the
worship of Ra-Horakhti under the name of Aton
had made great strides towards supremacy, there
is as yet no sign of the lofty monotheism which
the Pharaoh was soon to propound.

In the portions of the tomb of Horemheb which
date from this period, Ra-Horakhti is invoked
in the following words: "Ra-Horakhti, great
god, Lord of heaven, Lord of earth, who cometh
forth from his horizon and illuminateth the
Two Lands [of Egypt], the sun of darkness
as the great one, as Ra;" and again: "Ra,

Lord of Truth, great god, sovereign of Heliopolis,
. . . Horakhti, only god, king of the gods, who
rises in the west and sendeth forth his beauty."
From other sources, which we have seen, the
god is called " Ra - Horakhti rejoicing in the
horizon in his name Heat-which-is-in-Aton."

Here we have simply the old religion of
Heliopolis, to which has been grafted something of the doctrines of the Syrian Adonis
or Aton.   At Heliopolis there was a sacred
bull, known as Mnevis, which was regarded as the
living personification of Ra-Horakhti, and which
was treated with divine honours, like the more
famous Apis bull of Memphis.   Even this superstition was accepted by the king at this time,
and continued to be acknowledged by him for
yet another year or two.[1] The " Heat-which-is-
in-Aton " offered food for much speculation, and,
by directing the attention to an intangible quality
of the sun, opened up the widest fields for religious
thought.   But, with this exception, there was
nothing as yet in the new religion to command
one's admiration.

[1] Is there a distant connection between Mnevis and the Minoan
bull of Crete ? See p. 183.

III.

AKHNATON FOUNDS A NEW CITY.

"A brave soul, undauntedly facing the momentum of immemorial tradition . . . that he might disseminate ideas far beyond and above the capacity of his age to understand."—BREASTED : 'History of Egypt.'

---

1. THE BREAK WITH THE PRIESTHOOD
OF AMON-RA.

THE expected break with the priesthood of
Amon was not long in coming. One knows
nothing of the details of the quarrel, but it
may be supposed that Akhnaton himself flung
down the gauntlet, making the rash attempt
to rid himself of the weight of an organisation
which had proved such a drag upon his actions.
There is no evidence to show that he dis-
banded the priesthood, or prohibited the worship
of Amon at this period of his reign ; but as
the ultimate persecution of that god, some

years later, commenced very soon after the
death of his mother, one may suppose that
it was her restraining influence which prevented
him from precipitating a struggle to the death
with the god of Thebes. The king was now
entering upon the sixth year of his reign and
the seventeenth of his age, and he was already
developing in his mind theories and principles
which were soon to. produce radical changes in
the new religion of the Court. He found, no
doubt, that it was hopeless to attempt to
convert the people of Thebes to the new
doctrines; and daily he realised the more
clearly that the development either of the
faith of Ra-Horakhti Aton, or of the ideals
which he was beginning to find therein,
was cramped and checked by the hostility
of the influences which pressed around his
immediate circle. From the walls of every
temple, from pylons and gateways, pillars and
obelisks, the figure of Amon stared down at
him in defiance; and everywhere he was confronted with the tokens of that god's power.
His little temple at Karnak was overshadowed
by the larger buildings of Amon; and the

few priests who served at the new altar were
lost amidst the crowds of the ministers of the
Theban god. How could the flower thrive
and bloom in such uncongenial soil? How could
the sun shine through such density of conventional tradition?

The king, no doubt, endeavoured to cripple
the priesthood of Amon by cutting down its
budget as much as possible, and by attempting to win over to his side some of the
priests of high standing. Had he succeeded in
reducing it to the rank of the smaller cults,
it is probable that he would have been satisfied so to leave it; for at this time he wished
only to place Ra-Horakhti in a position of
undoubted supremacy above all other gods.
But the vast resources of Amon seemed un-
conquerable, and there appeared to be little
chance of reducing the priesthood to a position
of inferior rank.

In this dilemma the king took a step
which had been for some time considered
in his mind and in the minds of his advisers.
He decided to abandon Thebes. He would
build a city far away from all contaminating

influences, and there he would hold his court and worship his god. . On clean, new soil, he would establish the earthly home of Ra-Horakhti Aton, and there, with his faithful followers, he would develop those schemes which now so filled his brain.   Thus also, by reducing Thebes to the position of a provincial town, he might lessen the power of the priesthood of Amon; for no longer would Amon be the royal god, the god of the capital. He would shake the dust of Thebes from off his sandals, and never again would he allow himself to be baffled and irritated by the sight of the glories of Amon.

The first step which he took was that of changing his name from Amonhotep, "The-Peace-of-Amon," to Akhnaton, "The-Glory-of-Aton"; and from that time forth the word Amon hardly passed his lips.   He retained two of his other names,—i.e., "Beautiful-is-the-being-of-Ra," and "The-Only-One-of-Ra," the latter being often used by him; but such titles and names as that which made mention of Karnak he entirely dispensed with.   He now laid more stress upon the nature of his god as "Aton" or "the Aton"[1] than as Ra-Horakhti; and from this time onwards the name Ra-Horakhti becomes less and less prominent, though retained throughout the king's reign.

2. AKHNATON SELECTS THE SITE OF HIS CITY.

Down the river it would seem that the young Pharaoh now sailed in his royal *dahabiyeh*, looking to right and left as he went, now inspecting this site and now examining that. At last he came upon a place which suited his fancy to perfection. It was situated about 160 miles above the modern Cairo. At this point the limestone cliffs upon the east bank leave the river and recede for about three miles, returning to the water some five or six miles farther along. Thus a bay is formed which is protected on its west side by the river in which there here lies a small island, and in all other directions by the crescent of the

---

[1] The god is sometimes called "Aton" simply, and sometimes *Pa Aton*, "the Aton"; just as we speak of "Christ" or "the Christ," and of "Lord" or "the Lord," this latter being the actual meaning of "Aton."

cliffs.   Upon the island he would erect pavilions
and pleasure-houses.   Along the edge of the river
there was a narrow strip of cultivated land whereon he would plant his palace gardens, and those
of the nobles' villas.   Behind this verdant band
the smooth desert stretched, and here he would
build the palace itself and the great temples.
Behind this again, the sand and gravel surface
of the wilderness gently sloped up to the foot
of the cliffs, and here there would be roads and
causeways whereon the chariots might be whirled
in the early mornings.   In the face of the cliffs
he would cut his tomb and those of his followers;
and at intervals around the crescent of these
hills he would cause great boundary stones to
be made, so that all men might know and
respect the limits of his city.   What splendid
quays would edge the river, what palaces reflect
their whiteness in its waters!   There would be
broad shaded avenues, and shimmering lakes surrounded by the fairest trees of Asia.   Temples
would raise their lofty pylons to the blue skies,
and broad courts should lie stretched in the
sunlight.

In Akhnaton's youthful mind there already

stood the temples and the mansions; already he heard the sound of sweet music. The laughter of maidens was added to the singing of the birds which he heard in the trees; the pomp of imperial Egypt displaced the farm-houses and the fields of corn which now occupied the site; and the song of the shepherd in the wilderness was changed to the rolling psalms of the Aton. Fair was this dream and enthralling to the dreamer. To Queen Tiy it probably did not appeal so strongly; for Thebes was full of associations to her, and her palace beside the lake was very dear. There is, indeed, every reason to suppose that the dowager-queen lived on at Thebes after her son had abandoned it.

3. THE FIRST FOUNDATION INSCRIPTION.

Preparations were soon made for the laying out of the city, and in a very short time Akhnaton was called upon to visit the site in order to perform the foundation ceremonies. Fortunately the inscriptions upon some of the boundary tablets in the desert tell us something of the manner in which the king marked the limits of the city.[1] The first inscription reads as follows :—

Year 6, fourth month of the second season, day 13.[2] . . . On this day the King was in the City of the Horizon of Aton.[3] His Majesty ascended a great chariot of electrum, [appearing] like Aton when he rises from his [eastern] horizon and fills the land with his love ; and he started a goodly course [from his camping place] to the City of the Horizon. . . . Heaven was joyful, earth was glad, and every heart was happy when they saw him. And his Majesty offered a great sacrifice to Aton, of bread, beer, horned bulls, polled bulls, beasts, fowl, wine, incense, frankincense, and all goodly herbs on this day of demarcating the City of the Horizon. . . .

After these things, the good pleasure of Aton being done, . . . [the King returned from] the City of the Horizon, and he rested upon his great throne with which he is well pleased, which

---

[1] The translation here given is based upon that published by Davies in Amarna V. ; but the year cannot be the fourth, as there stated as probable, since in the above-mentioned letter dated in year 5 the king is still called Amonhotep, whereas in this inscription he is called Akhnaton.

[2] The day is not certain ; perhaps it is day 4.

[3] For the sake of brevity it is often called "the City of the Horizon," simply, in this volume.

uplifts his beauties. And his Majesty continued
in the presence of his father Aton, and Aton
shone upon him in life and length of days,
invigorating his body each day.

And his Majesty said, "Bring me the companions of the King, the great ones and the
mighty ones, the captains of soldiers, and the
nobles of the land in its entirety." And they
were conducted to him straightway, and they
lay on their bellies before his Majesty, kissing
the ground before his mighty will.

And his Majesty said unto them, "Ye behold
the City of the Horizon of Aton, which the
Aton has desired me to make for him as a
monument in the great name of my Majesty
for ever. For it was the Aton, my father,
that brought me to this City of the Horizon.
There was not a noble who directed me to it;
there was not any man in the whole land
who led me to it, saying, 'It is fitting for his
Majesty that he make a City of the Horizon
of Aton in this place.' Nay, but it was the
Aton, my father, that directed me to it to
make it for him. . . . Behold the Pharaoh found
that [this site] belonged not to a god, nor to
a goddess, it belonged not to a prince, nor to
a princess. There was no right for any man
to act as owner of it." . . .

[. . . And they answered and said] "Lo !
it is Aton that putteth [the thought] in thy
heart regarding any place that he desires. He

doth not uplift the name of any King except thy Majesty; he doth not [exalt] any other except [thee.] „ . . Thou drawest unto Aton every land, thou adornest for him the towns which he had made for his own self, all lands, all countries, the Hanebu[1] with their products and their tribute upon their backs for him that made their life, and by whose rays one lives and breathes the air. May he grant eternity in seeing his rays. . . . Verily, the City of the Horizon will thrive like Aton in heaven for ever and ever."

Then his Majesty lifted his hand to heaven unto Him that formed him, saying, "As my father Ra-Horakhti Aton liveth, the great and living Aton, ordaining life, vigorous in life, my father, my rampart of a million cubits, my re-membrancer of eternity, my witness of that which pertains to eternity, who formeth himself with his own hands, whom no artificer hath known, who is established in rising and in set-ting each day without ceasing. Whether he is in heaven or in earth,[2] every eye seeth him without [failing,] while he fills the land with his beams and makes every face to live. With seeing whom may my eyes be satisfied daily, when he rises in this temple of Aton in the City of the Horizon, and fills it with his own self by his beams, beauteous in love, and ˙lays

---

[1] Mediterranean people.

[2] This has reference to the rays which come from the Aton.

them upon me in life and length of days for
ever and ever. -

"I will make the City of the Horizon of
Aton for the Aton, my father, in this place. I
will not make the City south of it, north of it,
west of it, or east of it. I will not pass beyond
the southern boundary - stone southward, neither
will I pass beyond the northern boundary-stone
northward to make for him a City of the Horizon
there; neither will I make for him a city on
the western side. Nay, but I will make the
City of the Horizon for the Aton, my father,
upon the east side, the place which he did
enclose for his own self with cliffs, and made
a plain (?) in the midst of it that I might sacrifice to him thereon: this is it. Neither shall
the Queen say unto me, 'Behold, there is a
goodly place for the City of the Horizon in
another place,' and I hearken unto her. Neither
shall any noble nor [any one] of all men who
are in the whole land [say unto me], 'Behold,
there is a goodly place for the City of the
Horizon in another place,' and I hearken unto
them. Whether it be down-stream or southwards,
or westwards, or eastwards, I will not say 'I
will abandon this City of the Horizon and will
hasten away and make the City of the Horizon
in this other goodly place' for ever. Nay,
but I did find this City of the Horizon for
the Aton, which he had himself desired, and
with which he is pleased for ever and ever.

"I will make a temple of Aton for the Aton, my father, in this place. I will make a . . . of Aton for the Aton, my father, in this place. I will make a Shadow-of-the-Sun [1] of the Great Wife of the King, Nefertiti, for the Aton, my father, in this place. I will make a House of Rejoicing for the Aton, my father, on the island of 'Aton illustrious in Festivals' in this place. . . . I will make all works which are necessary for the Aton, my father, in this place. I will make . . . for the Aton, my father, in this place. I will make for myself the Palace of Pharaoh; and I will make the Palace of the Queen in this place. There shall be made for me a sepulchre in the eastern hills; my burial shall be made therein . . . and the burial of the Chief Wife of the King, Nefertiti, shall be made therein, and the burial of the King's daughter Merytaton shall be made therein. If I die in any town of the north, south, west, or east, I will be brought here and my burial shall be made in the City of the Horizon. If the Great Queen, Nefertiti, who lives, die in any town of the north, south, west, or east, she shall be brought here and buried in the City of the Horizon. If the King's daughter Merytaton die in any town of the north, south, west, or east, she shall be brought here and buried in the City of the Horizon. And the sepulchre of Mnevis shall be made in the

---

[1] This seems to have been a temple.

eastern hills and he shall be buried therein. The
tombs of the High Priests and the Divine Fathers
and the priests of the Aton shall be made in
the eastern hills, and they shall be buried therein.
The tombs of the officers, and others, shall be
made in the eastern hills, and they shall be
buried therein.

" For as my father Ra-Horakhti Aton liveth . . .
[the words ?] of the priests, more evil are they
than those things which I heard until the year
four, more evil are they than those things which
I have heard in . . . more evil are they than
those things which King [Nebmaara [1]] heard,
more evil are they than those things which
Menkheperura [2] heard. . . ."

The rest of the inscription is so much broken
that only a few words here and there can be
read. They seem to refer to the king's further
projects,—how he will make ships to sail to and
from the city, how he will build granaries, cele-
brate festivals, plant trees, and so on.

The reference to the year four is very interesting, and it would seem that it was at about
that date that the king's eyes were opened to
the necessity of making war upon the priesthood

---

[1] The second name of Amonhotep III., Akhnaton's father.
[2] The second name of Thothmes IV., Akhnaton's grandfather.

of Amon. As we have seen, it was in about the fourth year of his reign that the great changes in the art took place, and the symbol of the sun's rays was introduced into the sculptures. The mention of the two previous Pharaohs shows that troubles were already brewing then; but it had remained for the energetic young Akhnaton to bring matters to a head.

4. THE SECOND FOUNDATION INSCRIPTION.

The inscription recording these events was probably not written until some months after they had occurred. Just when the engravers had made an end of their work a second daughter was born to the king and queen, whom they named Meketaton; and orders were given that her figure should be added upon the boundary tablet beside that of her sister, which already appeared there with Akhnaton and Nefertiti. The king was somewhat distressed that a son had not been granted to him; for the thought was bitter that, in the event of his death, all his projects would fall to the ground. He therefore altered the wording of the inscriptions about to be written on the other boundary tablets; and, by including his oath in the text, he added an even greater integrity to the decree. The name of the second daughter was now inserted in this inscription, which reads :—

Year six, fourth month of the second season, thirteenth day.

On this day the King was in the City of the Horizon of Aton, in the parti-coloured tent made for his Majesty in the City of the Horizon, the name of which is "The Aton is well pleased." And his Majesty ascended a great chariot of electrum, drawn by a span of horses, and [he appeared] like Aton when he rises from the horizon and fills the two lands with his love. And he started a goodly course to the City of the Horizon, on this the first occasion, . . . to dedicate it as a monument to the Aton, even as his father Ra-Horakhti Aton had given command. . . . And he caused a great sacrifice to be offered.

And his Majesty went southward, and halted on his chariot before his father Ra-Horakhti Aton, at the [foot of the] south-east hills, and Aton shone upon him in life and length of days, invigorating his body every day.

Now this is the oath pronounced by the King:—
"As my father Ra-Horakhti Aton liveth, as my heart is happy in the Queen and her children—as to whom may it be granted that the Chief Wife of the King, Nefertiti, living for ever and ever, grow aged after a multitude of years, in the care of the Pharaoh, and may it be granted that the King's daughter Merytaton and the King's daughter Meketaton, her children, grow old in the care of the Chief Wife of the King, their mother. . . .

"This is my oath of truth which it is my desire to pronounce, and of which I will not say 'It is false' eternally for ever.

"The southern boundary-stone which is on the eastern hills. It is the boundary-stone of the City of the Horizon, namely this one by which I have made halt. I will not pass beyond it southwards for ever and ever. Make the south-west boundary-stone opposite it on the western hills of the City of the Horizon exactly.

"The middle boundary-stone which is on the eastern hills. It is the boundary-stone of the City of the Horizon by which I have made halt on the eastern hills of the City of the Horizon. I will not pass beyond it eastwards for ever and ever. Make the middle boundary-stone which is to be on the western hills opposite it exactly.

"The north-eastern boundary-stone by which I have made halt. It is the northern boundary-stone of the City of the Horizon. I will not pass beyond it down-stream for ever and ever. Make the north boundary-stone which is to be on the western hills opposite it exactly.

" And the City of the Horizon of Aton extends from the south boundary-stone as far as the north boundary-stone, measured between boundary-stone and boundary-stone on the eastern, hills [which measurement] amounts to 6 *ater*,[1] ¾ *khe*, and 4 cubits. Likewise from the south-west boundary-stone to the north-west boundary-stone on the western hills [the measurement] amounts to 6 *ater*, ¾ *khe*, and 4 cubits likewise exactly.

" And the area within these four boundary-stones from the eastern hills to the western hills is the City of the Horizon of Aton in its proper self. It belongs to my father Ra-Horakhti Aton: mountains, deserts, meadows, islands, high-ground, low-ground, land, water, villages, embankments, men, beasts, groves, and all things which the Aton my father shall bring into existence for ever and ever.

" I will not neglect this oath which I have made to the Aton my father for ever and ever; nay, but it shall be set on a tablet of stone as the south-east boundary, likewise as the northeast boundary of the City of the Horizon; and it shall be set likewise on a tablet of stone as the south-west boundary, likewise as the north-west boundary of the City of the Horizon. It shall not be erased, it shall not be washed out, it shall

---

[1] The *ater* corresponds to the Greek *schoinos*, and the *khe* is the *schoenium* of 100 cubits, 40 *khe* making one *ater*.

not be kicked, it shall not be struck with stones, its spoiling shall not be brought about. If it be missing, if it be spoilt, if the tablet on which it is shall fall, I will renew it again afresh in the place in which it was."

5. THE DEPARTURE FROM THEBES.

From the above inscription one sees that Akhnaton had now decided to include the west bank of the river, opposite to the original site, in the new domain; and the great boundary tablets are there to be found as on the eastern side. By the time these decrees were engraved the Pharaoh was nearly eighteen years of age; and these developments in his plans are the natural signs of the progress of his brain towards that of a grown man.

Having laid the foundations of the city, the king probably returned to Thebes, where he waited as patiently as possible for his dream to take concrete form. This period of waiting must have been peculiarly trying to him, for his troubles with the Amon priesthood must have embittered his days. He seems, however, to have been extremely devoted to his wife, Nefertiti, who had now grown, it would seem, into a beautiful young woman of fifteen or sixteen years of age; and the arrival of the second baby afforded an interest which meant much to him. One may now picture the king and queen living, in the seclusion of the palace, a homely, simple existence, ever dwelling in a happy day-dream upon the future glories of the new city, and the rising power of the religion of Aton. Akhnaton's ill-health, of course, must have caused both his friends and himself much anxiety; but even this had its compensations, for those who suffer from epilepsy are by the gods beloved, and Akhnaton, no doubt, believed the hallucinations due to his disease to be god-given visions. There must have been a very considerable amount of business to be worked through in connection with the building of the city, and he could have had little time to brood upon what he now considered to be the wrongs inflicted upon him and his house by the priests of Amon.

So passed the seventh year of his reign

without any particular records to mark it.
At Aswan there is a monument which perhaps
dates from about this period. The king's
chief sculptor, Bek, was there employed in
obtaining red granite for the decoration of
the new city; and he caused to be made
upon a large rock a commemorative tablet.
On it one sees him before Akhnaton, whose
figure has been erased at a later date; and
the altar of the Aton, above which are the
usual sun's rays, stands beside them. Bek calls
himself "The Chief of the Works in the Red
[Granite] Hills, the assistant whom his Majesty
himself taught, Chief of the Sculptors on
the great and mighty monuments of the
King in the house of Aton in the City of
the Horizon of Aton." Here also one sees
Men, the father of Bek, who was also Chief
of the Sculptors, presenting an offering to a
statue of Amonhotep III., under whom he had
served.

The eighth year of Akhnaton's reign, and the
nineteenth year of his age, was memorable, for
it would seem that he now took up his permanent
residence in the City of the Horizon. On some

of the boundary tablets a repetition of the royal oath is recorded; and, as this is the last mention of *a visit* made by Akhnaton to the new capital, one may suppose that henceforth he was resident there. The inscription reads :—

> This oath (of the sixth year) was repeated in year eight, first month of the second season, eighth day. The King was in the City of the Horizon of Aton, and Pharaoh stood mounted on a great chariot of electrum, inspecting the boundary-stones of the Aton. . . .

Then follows a list of these boundary-stones, and the inscription ends with the words :—

> And the breadth of the City of the Horizon of Aton is from cliff to cliff, from the eastern horizon of heaven to the western horizon of heaven. It shall be for my father Ra-Horakhti Aton, its hills, its deserts, all its fowl, all its people, all its cattle, all things which the Aton produces, on which his rays shine, all things which are in . . . the City of the Horizon, they shall be for the father, the living Aton, unto the temple of Aton in the City of the Horizon for ever and ever; they are all offered to his spirit. And may his rays be beauteous when they receive them.

Thus was the king's city planned and laid

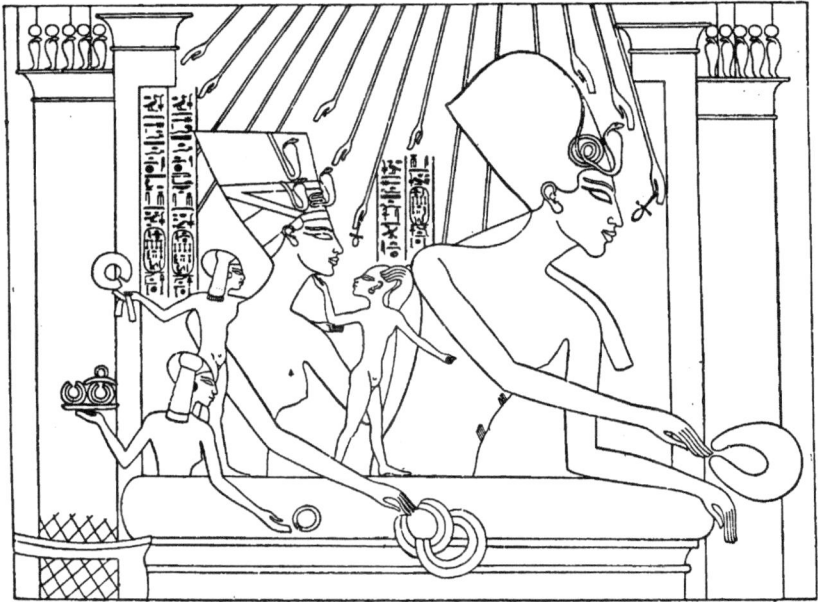

Akhnaton and Nefertiti with their three Daughters.

out. The two years of feverish work had
probably produced considerable results, and
already we may picture the city taking form.
The royal palace was perhaps almost finished
by now, and the villas of some of the nobles
were habitable. With many a sigh of relief
Akhnaton must have bade farewell to Thebes. A
third daughter, who was named Ankhsenpaaton,
had just been born; and one may thus picture
the royal party which sailed down the river
as being very distinctly a family. One sees
Akhnaton, a sickly young man of nineteen years
of age, walking to and fro upon the deck of the
royal vessel, with his hand upon the shoulder
of his fair young wife, now some seventeen years
old, in whose arms the baby princess is carried.
Toddling beside them are the two other princesses,
one somewhat over two years of age, the other
about four years. The queen's sister, Nezemmut,
records of whose existence soon become apparent, was perhaps also of the party, having left the
court of Mitanni to be a companion to Nefertiti.
Ay and Ty, the foster-parents of Nefertiti, were
doubtless with the royal family now as they
sailed down the river; and several of the nobles

who play a part in the following pages no doubt formed the suite which attended to the royal commands.

6. THE AGE OF AKHNATON.

We have spoken of the king as being nineteen years old. The story has now reached a point at which we must pause to consider this vexed question of Akhnaton's age. In the above pages it has been said that the Pharaoh was about eleven years old at his marriage and accession to the throne; was fifteen when the canons of art were changed and the symbols of the Aton religion introduced; was seventeen when the foundations of the new city were laid; and was nineteen when he took up his residence there. Let us study these ages in the above order.

Firstly, then, as to the king's marriage. The mummy of Thothmes IV., the grandfather of Akhnaton, has been shown by Dr Elliot Smith to be that of a man not more than about twenty-six years of age. That king was succeeded by

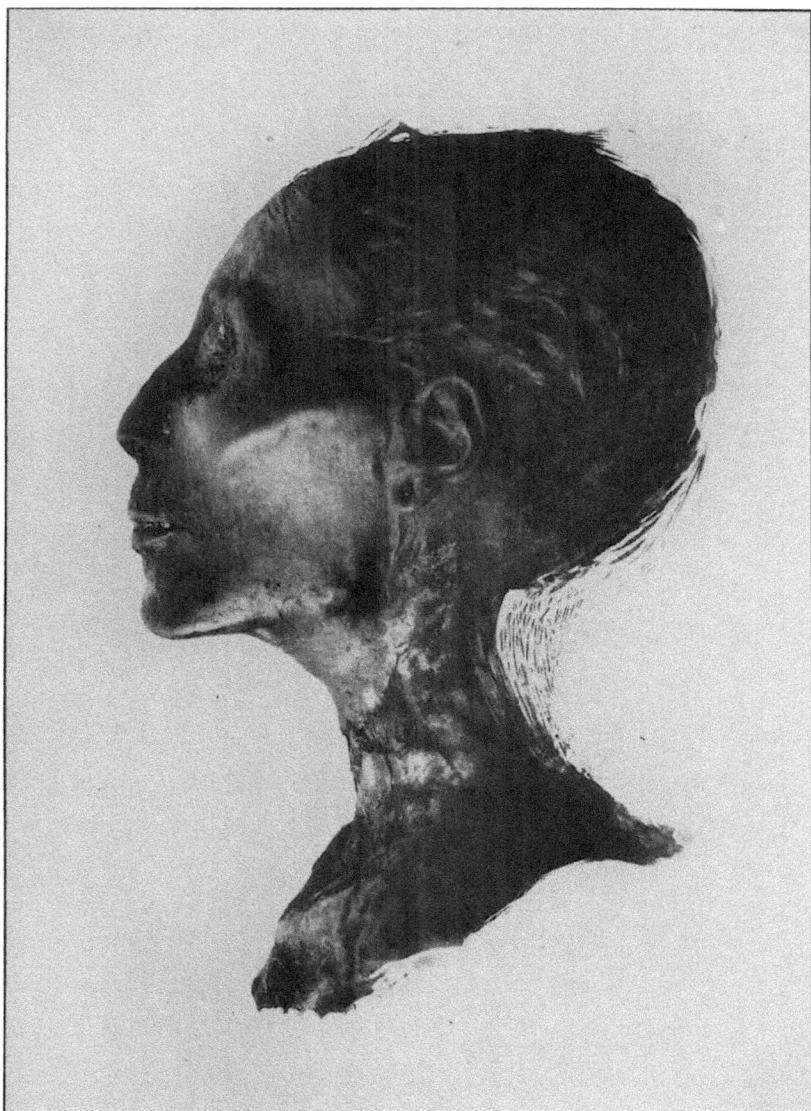

The Head of the Mummy of Thothmes IV., the grandfather of Akhnaton.

his son Amonhotep III., who is known to have been married to Queen Tiy before the second year of his reign, and to have been old enough at that time to begin to hunt big game. It would be difficult to believe that he would be permitted to join any hunting party, however secure against accident, before the twelfth year of his age; but, on the other hand, if he was more than that age, his father would have to have been less than twelve at *his* marriage. Thus the only possible conclusion is that both Thothmes IV. and Amonhotep III. were barely thirteen when they were married, and very possibly even younger. This is shown to be a correct conclusion by the fact that the mummy of Amonhotep III. has been pronounced by Dr Elliot Smith to be that of a man of forty-five or fifty; and as he reigned thirty-six years he must have been *at most* fourteen, and probably some years younger, at his accession and marriage.

There is not sufficient evidence to show at what ages the previous Pharaohs of the dynasty had married, but as Akhnaton's father and grandfather entered into matrimony at this early age, it would not be safe to suppose that he himself delayed his marriage till a later age. Queen Tiy was in all probability married when she was ten or eleven years old.[1] Akhnaton's daughter Merytaton, who was born in the fourth or fifth year of his reign, was, as will be seen in due course, married before the seventeenth year of the reign—that is to say, when she was twelve or younger. The Princess Ankhsenpaaton, who was born in the eighth year, was married, at latest, two years after Akhnaton's death—i.e., when she was eleven. Another of Akhnaton's daughters, Nefernefernaton, who has not yet appeared, was born in her father's eleventh year and was married before the fifteenth, and therefore could only have been four or five years of age.

Child-marriages such as these are common in Egypt, even at the present day. Those who have lived on the Nile, and have studied the national habits, will assuredly fix the probable age of a royal *mariage de convenance* at about thirteen years, and will agree that eleven and twelve are also highly likely ages.

Secondly, as to Akhnaton's age at the

[1] See note on p. 178.

changing of the art. In the biography of
Bakenkhonsu, the High Priest of Amon under
Rameses II., that official tells us that he arrived
at the state of manhood at the age of sixteen,
and one may therefore suppose that this was
the recognised legal age at which a man became
a responsible agent in Egypt. Now it has
been clearly seen that Akhnaton was under the
regency of his mother during the first years
of his reign, and mention has been made of
the inscription at Wady Hammamat, where,
although the new symbol of the religion is
shown, Queen Tiy's name is placed beside that
of her son in an equally honourable position.
She was thus still Queen Regent when the art
was changed, and her son could not yet have
come of age—*i.e.*, he must then have been under
sixteen.

Thirdly, we have to consider the question
of his age when he laid the foundations of the
new city. This was the first decisive action
performed by the king in which his mother
has no concern, and of which she perhaps even
disapproved, and it surely marks the period
at which he took the government into his

H

own hands. If, like Bakenkhonsu, he came of age at sixteen, in the fifth year of his reign, the founding of the new capital in the following year would well fit in with the supposition that the abandoning of Thebes marks the date of the king's arrival at maturity.

It may be asked how so young a person could conceive that great dream of the new city dedicated to the Aton. But, after all, he was seventeen years of age when the idea came to him, nineteen when he had properly developed the plan, and perhaps as much as twenty when he took up his residence there. Akhnaton's greatness, as will be seen later, dates from the height of his reign in the City of the Horizon, and not from his early years. Still, when one calls to mind the infant prodigies, the child preachers who stir an audience at the age of twelve, one may credit a boy of sixteen or seventeen with the planning of a new city. Even in the cold Occident such youthful wiseacres are not rare, and surely they blossom forth less infrequently in the maturing warmth of the Orient.

IV.

AKHNATON FORMULATES THE RELIGION OF ATON.

"No such grand theology had ever appeared in the world before, so far as we know; and it is the forerunner of the later monotheist religions." —PETRIE: 'The Religion of Ancient Egypt.'

1. ATON THE TRUE GOD.

AMIDST the fair palaces and verdant gardens of the new city, Akhnaton, now a man of some twenty years, turned his thoughts fully to the development of his religion. It is necessary, therefore, for us to glance at the essential features of this the most enlightened doctrine of the ancient world, and in some degree to make ourselves acquainted with the creed which the king himself was evolving out of that worship of Ra-Horakhti Aton in which he had been educated.

Originally the Aton was the actual sun's disk;
but, as has been said, the god was now called
"Heat-which-is-in-Aton," and Akhnaton, con-
centrating his attention on this aspect of the
godhead, drew the eyes of his followers towards
a force far more intangible and distant than
the dazzling orb to which they bowed down.
Akhnaton's conception of God, as we now begin
to observe it, was as the power which created
the sun, the energy which penetrated to this
earth in the sun's heat and caused all things
to grow. At the present day the scientist will
tell you that God is the ultimate source of life,
that where natural explanation fails there God
is to be found: He is, in a word, the author
of energy, the primal motive-power of all known
things. Akhnaton, centuries upon centuries before the birth of the scientist, defined God in
just this manner. In an age when men believed,
as some do still, that a deity was but an exaggerated creature of this earth, having a form
built on material lines, this youthful Pharaoh
proclaimed God to be the formless essence,
the intelligent germ, the loving force, which
permeated time and space. Let it be clearly

understood that the Aton as conceived by the
young Pharaoh was in no sense one of those
old deities which our God ultimately replaced
in Egypt. The Aton is God as we conceive
Him. There is no quality attributed by the
king to the Aton which we do not attribute
to our God. Like a flash of blinding light in
the night - time the Aton stands out for a
moment amidst the black Egyptian darkness,
and disappears once more, — the first signal to
this world of the future religion of the West.
No man whose mind is free from prejudice will
fail to see a far closer resemblance to the teachings of Christ in the religion of Akhnaton than
in that of Abraham, Isaac, and Jacob. The
faith of the patriarchs is the lineal ancestor
of the Christian faith; but the creed of Akhnaton is its isolated prototype. One might believe
that Almighty God had for a moment revealed
himself to Egypt, and had been more clearly,
though more momentarily, interpreted there than
ever He was in Syria or Palestine before the
time of Christ.

2. ATON THE TENDER FATHER OF ALL CREATION.

Amon-Ra and the old gods of Egypt were, for the most part, but deified mortals, endued with monstrous, though limited, powers, and still having around them traditions of aggrandised human deeds. Others, we have seen, had their origin in natural phenomena : the wind, the Nile, the starry heavens, and the like. All were terrific or revengeful, if so they had a mind to be, and all were able to be moved by human emotions. But to Akhnaton, although he had absolutely no precedent upon which to launch his thoughts, God was the intangible and yet ever-present Father of mankind, made manifest in sunshine. The youthful high priest called upon his subjects to search for their God not in the confusion of battle or behind the smoke of human sacrifices, but amidst the flowers and the trees, amidst the wild duck and the fishes. He preached an enlightened nature - study : in some respects he was, perhaps, the first apostle of the Simple Life.

He strove to break down conventional thought, and ceaselessly he urged his people to worship "in truth," simply, without an excess of ceremonial. While the elder gods had been apparent in natural convulsions and in the more awful incidents of life, Akhnaton's kindly father could be seen in the little details of existence, in the growing poppies, in the soft wind which filled the sails of the ships, in the fish which leapt from the river. Like a greater than he, Akhnaton taught his disciples to address their maker as their "Father which art in Heaven." The Aton was the joy which caused the young sheep "to dance upon their legs," and the birds "to flutter in their marshes." He was the god of the simple pleasures of life; and although Akhnaton himself was indeed a man of sorrows, plenteously acquainted with grief, happiness was the watchword which he gave to his followers.

Akhnaton did not permit any graven image to be made of the Aton. The True God, said the king, had no form; and he held to this opinion throughout his life. The symbol of the religion was the sun's disk, from which there extended numerous rays, each ray ending in a hand; but this symbol was not worshipped. To Christians, in the same way, the cross is the symbol of their creed; but the cross itself is not worshipped. Never before had man conceived a formless deity, a god who was not endowed with the five human senses. The Hebrew patriarchs believed God to be capable of walking in a garden in the cool of the evening, to have made man in his own image, to be possessed of face, form, and hinder parts. But Akhnaton, stemming with his hand the flood of tradition, boldly proclaimed God to be a life-giving, intangible essence: the *heat* which is in the sun. He was "the living Aton,"—that is to say, the power which produced and sustained the energy and movement of the sun. Although he was so often called "the Aton," he was more closely defined as "the Master of the Aton."[1] The flaming glory of the sun was the most practical symbol of the godhead, and the warm rays of sunshine constituted the most obvious connection between heaven and earth; but always Akhnaton attempted to raise the eyes of the thinkers beyond this visible or understandable expression

---

[1] Davies, Amarna, I. 45.

of divinity, to strain them upwards in the effort
to discern that which was "behind the veil."
In lighting on a motive power more remote
than the sun, and acting through the sun,
the young Pharaoh may be said to have penetrated as far behind the eternal barrier as one
may ever hope to penetrate this side the church-
yard.   But though so remote, the Aton was
the tender, loving Father of all men, ever-
present and ever-mindful of his creatures.   There
dropped not a sigh from the lips of a babe
that the intangible Aton did not hear; no lamb
bleated for its mother but the remote Aton
hastened to soothe it.   He was the loving
"Father and Mother of all that He had
made," who "brought up millions by His bounty."

The destructive qualities of the sun were never
referred to, and that pitiless orb under which
Egypt sweats and groans for the summer months
each year had nothing in common with the gentle
Father conceived by Akhnaton.   The Aton was
"the Lord of Love."   He was the tender nurse
who "creates the man - child in woman, and
soothes him that he may not weep"; whose
love, to use an Egyptian phrase of exquisite

tenderness, "makes the hands to faint." His
beams were "beauteous with love" as they fell
upon His people and upon His city, "very rich
in love." "Thy love is great and large," says
one of Akhnaton's psalms. "Thou fillest the
two lands of Egypt with Thy love;" and
another passage runs: "Thy rays encompass
the lands. . . . Thou bindest them with Thy
love."

Surely never in the history of the world had
man conceived a god who "so loved the world."
One may search the inscriptions in vain for any
reference to a malignant power, to vengeance,
to jealousy, or to hatred. The Hebrew psalmist
said of God, "Like as a father pitieth his
children, even so is the Lord merciful"; and
Akhnaton, many a century before those words
were written, attributed just such a nature to
the Aton. The Aton was compassionate, was
merciful, was gentle, was tender; He knew not
anger, and there was no wrath in Him. His
overflowing love reached down the paths of life
from mankind to the beasts of the field and to
the little flowers themselves. "All flowers blow,"
says one of Akhnaton's hymns, "and that which

grows on the soil thrives at. Thy dawning, O Aton. They drink their fill [of warmth] before Thy face. All cattle leap upon their feet ; the birds that were in the nest fly forth with joy ; their wings which were closed move quickly with praise to the living Aton."

One stands amazed as one reads in pompous Egypt of a god who listens " when the chicken crieth in the egg - shell," and gives him life, delighting that he should " chirp with all his might" when he is hatched forth ; who finds pleasure in causing " the birds to flutter in their marshes, and the sheep to dance upon their feet." For the first time in the history of man the real meaning of God, as we now understand it, had been comprehended ; and the idea of a beneficent Creator who, though remote, spiritual, and impersonal, could love each one of His creatures, great or small, had been grasped by this young Pharaoh. God's unspeakable goodness and loving-kindness were as clearly interpreted by Akhnaton as ever they have been by mortal man ; and the wonder of it lies in this, that Akhnaton had absolutely nothing to base his theories upon. He was, so far as we know, the first man to whom God revealed Himself as the passionless, all-loving essence of unqualified goodness.

3. ATON WORSHIPPED AT SUNRISE AND SUNSET.

In order to prevent the more ignorant of his disciples from worshipping the sun itself, Akhnaton seems to have selected the sunrise and the sunset as the two hours for ceremonial adoration; for then the light, the beauty, the tenderness, of the celestial phenomenon could be appreciated, and the awful majesty of the sun was not in great prominence. Akhnaton attempted to cultivate in his followers an appreciation of the gentle hues of daybreak and of evening; and he taught them to believe that the oft-mentioned "beauties" of the Aton were only to be fully understood at these times. In the gladness of sunrise and in the hush of the sunset, the emotions are most apt to be touched and moved; for in Egypt there is always praise in the heart in the cool opalescence of the dawn, and in the red dusk there is many and many a dream.

Phrases such as the following may be gleaned from Akhnaton's hymns : " Thy rising is beautiful in the horizon of heaven, O living Aton, who dispensest life ; shining from the eastern horizon of heaven, Thou fillest Egypt with Thy beauty." " Thy setting is beautiful, O living Aton, . . . who guidest . . . all countries that they may make laudations at Thy dawning and at Thy setting." " When the Aton rises all the land is in joy ; His rays produce eyes for all that He has created ; and men say, ' It is life to see Him, there is death in not seeing Him.' " " When Thou settest alive,[1] O Aton, West and East give praise to thee." " Thou settest behind the western horizon ; Thou settest in life and gladness, and every eye rejoices though they are in darkness after Thou settest." " When Thou hast risen they live ; when Thou settest they die."

The ceremonial side of the religion does not seem to have been complex. The priests, of whom there were very few, offered sacrifices, consisting mostly of vegetables, fruit, and flowers, to the Aton, and at these ceremonies the king

---

[1] The idea is that the Aton does not die as dies the sunlight.

and his family often officiated. They then sang
psalms and offered prayers, and, with much
sweet music, gave praise to the great Father of
joy and love. The Aton, however, was not
thought to delight in these ceremonies as He
did in more natural thanksgivings. Why should
God be praised in set phrases and studied poses
when all the fair world was shouting for the
joy of Him? The young calf frisking through
the poppy - covered meadows, the birds singing
upon the trees, the clouds racing across the
sky, were the true worshippers of God.

One of the recently discovered sayings of
Christ closely parallels Akhnaton's utterances.
"Ye ask," it runs, "who are those that draw
us to the kingdom if the kingdom is in heaven?
The fowls of the air, and all the beasts that
are under the earth or upon the earth, and the
fishes in the sea, these are they which draw
you, and the kingdom is within you." The
contemplation of nature was more to Akhnaton
than many ceremonies, and his thoughts were
more easily drawn upwards by the rustle of
the leaves than by the shaking of the systrum.

4. THE GOODNESS OF ATON.

In the gardens of the City of the Horizon Akhnaton was surrounded on all sides by the joyous beauties of nature. Here the birds sang merrily in the laden trees, here the cool north wind rustled through the leaves, setting them dancing upon their stems, here the many-coloured blossoms nodded to their reflections in the still lakes; and, as he watched the sun-light playing with the blue shadows, his heart seemed to fill to repletion with gratitude to God. "O Lord, how manifold are Thy works!" was his constant cry. "The whole land is in joy and holiday because of Thee. They shout to the height of heaven, they receive joy and gladness when they see Thee." How "fair of form" was the formless Aton, how "radiant of colour"! "All that Thou hast made," said the king, "leaps before Thee." "Thou makest the beauty of form through Thyself alone." "Eyes have life at sight of Thy beauty; hearts have health when the Aton shines."

As the psalmist sang, "The Lord is my

shepherd, I shall not want," so Akhnaton, in
the fulness of his heart, cried, "There is no
poverty for him who hath set Thee in his
heart; such an one cannot say, 'O, that I had.'"
"When Thou bringest life to men's hearts by Thy
beauty, there is indeed life." The Aton "gave
health to the eyes by His rays," and, "bright,
great, gleaming, high above all the earth," he
was "the cause of plenty,"—the very "food and
fatness of Egypt." To David, several centuries
later, God seemed to be "a strong tower of
defence"; and, thinking along the same lines,
Akhnaton called the Aton his "wall of brass of
a million cubits." The Aton was "the witness
of that which pertains to eternity," and to those
whose thoughts had strayed he was "the re-
membrancer of eternity." He was the "Lord
of Fate," the "Lord of Fortune," the "Master
of that which is ordained," the "Origin of
Fate," the "Chance which gives Life"; and in
so describing him Akhnaton reached a philosophical position which even to-day is quite
unassailable.

Unlike Jehovah, who was described as "great
above all other gods," the Aton was conceived

as being without rivals; and Akhnaton now never mentions the word "gods." "The living Aton beside whom there is no other," is one of the common phrases; and of Him again it is written, "Thou art alone, but infinite vitalities are in Thee by means of which to give life to Thy creatures."

Unlike Jehovah again, who was not infrequently thought to be a wrathful god, surrounded by clouds and darkness, and speaking through the roar of the thunders, the Aton was the "Lord of Peace," who could not tolerate battle and strife. Akhnaton was so opposed to war that he persistently refused to offer an armed resistance to the subsequent revolts which occurred in his Asiatic dominions. The Aton was a deity to whose tender heart human bloodshed made no appeal. In an age of martial glory, when the sword and buckler, the plumed helmet and the shirt of mail, glittered in every street and upon every highway, Akhnaton set himself in opposition to all heroics, and saw God without melodrama.

Above all things the Aton loved truth. Frankness, sincerity, straightforwardness, honesty, and veracity were qualities not always to be found in the heart of an Egyptian; and Akhnaton, in antagonism to the sins of hypocrisy and deception which he saw around him, always spoke of himself as "living in truth." "I have set truth in my inward parts," says one of his followers, "and falsehood is my loathing; for I know that the King rejoiceth in truth."

5. AKHNATON THE "SON OF GOD" BY TRADITIONAL RIGHT.

It may be understood how the boy longed for truth in all things when one remembers the thousand exaggerated conventions of Egyptian life at this time. Court etiquette had developed to a degree which rendered life to the Pharaoh an endless round of unnatural poses of mind and body. In the preaching of his doctrine of truth and simplicity Akhnaton did not fail to call upon his subjects to regard their Pharaoh not as a celestial god, as had been the custom, but as a man, though, of course, one of divine

Akhnaton driving with his Wife and Daughter.

origin.   It was usual for the Pharaoh to keep
aloof from his people : Akhnaton was to be
found in their midst.   The court demanded that
their lord should drive in solitary state through
the city : Akhnaton stood in his chariot with
his wife and children, and allowed the artist
to represent him joking therein with his little
daughter.   In portraying the Pharaoh the artist
was expected to draw him in some conventional
attitude of dignity : Akhnaton insisted upon
being shown in all manner of natural attitudes
—now leaning languidly upon a staff, now nurs-
ing his children, and now eating his dinner.
Thus again one sees his objection to heroics,
and his love of naturalness.

But while he strove for truth and sincerity
in this manner he did not attempt to remove
from his mind the belief in which he had been
brought up, that as Pharaoh of Egypt he was
himself partly divine.   Not only was he by
reason of his religion the representative, and
hence, in a manner of speech, the "son" of
God, but by right of royal descent he was the
"son of the Sun."   The names of the Pharaohs
were always surrounded by an oval band, known

as a cartouche, which was the distinguishing
mark of a royal name.   Akhnaton wrote the
name of the Aton within such an oval, thus
indicating that the Pharaoh's royal rights were
also held by, and therefore derived from, God
Himself.   There was thus, as Christ later taught
His disciples to believe, a kingdom of heaven
over which God presided; and although impersonal, intangible, and incomprehensible, the
Aton was the very "King of kings, the only
ruler of princes."   Amon-Ra and other of the
old deities had been called at various times
"King of the gods."   Akhnaton, however, applied
to Aton the words "King and God."

Akhnaton is spoken of as "the unique one
of Ra, whose beauties Aton created," and as
"the beloved son of Aton," whom "Aton bare."
Addressing the Aton, his courtiers were wont to
say, "Thy rays are on Thy bright image, the
Ruler of Truth (*i.e.*, the King), who proceeded
from eternity.   Thou givest to him Thy duration and Thy years; Thou hearkenest to all
that is in his heart, because Thou lovest him.
Thou makest him like the Aton, him Thy child,
the King."   "Thou lookest on him, for he pro-

ceeded[1] from Thee." "Thou hast placed him beside Thee for ever and ever, for he loves to gaze upon Thee. . . . Thou hast set him there till the swan shall turn black and the crow turn white, till the hills rise up to travel and the deeps rush into the rivers." "While heaven is, he shall be." Some of the Pharaohs had called themselves "the beautiful child of Amon"; and Akhnaton, borrowing this phrase, was sometimes spoken of as "the beautiful child of the Aton."[2]

In his capacity as Pharaoh and "son of God," Akhnaton demanded and received a very considerable amount of ceremonial homage; but he never blinded himself to the fact that he was primarily but a simple man. He most sincerely wished that his private life should be a worthy example to his subjects, and he earnestly desired that it should be observed in all its naturalness and simplicity. He did his utmost to elevate the position of women and the sanctity of the family by dis-

---

[1] Probably by royal descent is meant.

[2] In Egyptian this title reads *Pa shera nefer en pa Aton.* In the tomb of a certain Amonhotep, at El Assasîf, temp. Amonhotep III., the deceased Amonhotep I. is called *Pa shera nefer en Amon.*

playing to the world the ideal conditions of his
own married life. He made a point of caressing
his wife in public, putting his arm around her
neck in the sight of all men. As we have seen,
one of his forms of oath was, "As my heart is
happy in the Queen and her children. . . ."
He spoke of his wife always as "Mistress of
his happiness, . . . at hearing whose voice
the King rejoices." "Lady of grace" was she,
"great of love" and "fair of face." Every
wish that she expressed, declared Akhnaton,
was executed by him. Even on the most ceremonious occasions the queen sat beside her
husband and held his hand, while their children
frolicked around them; for such things pleased
that gentle father more than the savour of
burnt-offerings. It is seldom that the Pharaoh
is represented in the reliefs without his family;
and, in opposition to all tradition, the queen
is shown upon the same scale of size and importance as that of her husband. Akhnaton's
devotion to his children is very marked, and
he taught his disciples to believe that God
was the father, the mother, the nurse, and
the friend of the young. Thus, though "son

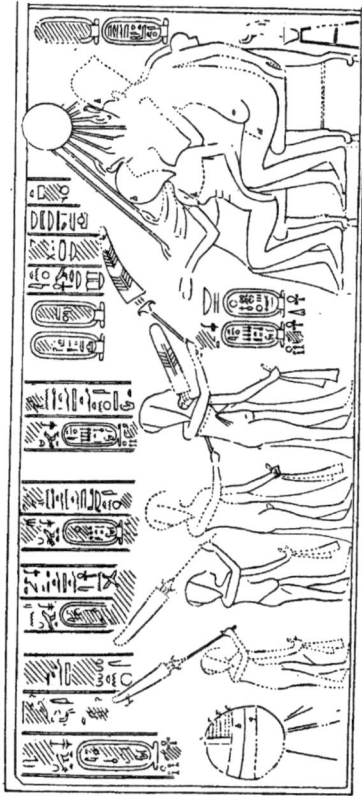

Akhnaton and his Wife and Children.

of God," Akhnaton preached the beauty of the human family, and laid stress on the sanctity of marriage and parenthood.

6. THE CONNECTIONS OF THE ATON WORSHIP WITH OLDER RELIGIONS.

In developing his religion Akhnaton must have come into almost daily conflict with the priesthoods of the old gods of Egypt; and even the Heliopolitan Ra-Horakhti, from which his own faith had been evolved, now fell far short of his ideals. He does not seem, however, to have yet imposed the worship of the Aton upon the provinces, nor to have persecuted the various priesthoods. He hoped, no doubt, that he would be able to persuade the whole country to his views as soon as those views were thoroughly matured; and, secure in his new city, he was free to purge his religion of its faults before declaring all other creeds illegal.

It is probable that the sacred bull, Mnevis, was banished from his ceremonies at an early date, for no tombs seem to have been made for these holy creatures, and they are not referred to after the sixth year of the king's reign. The priests of Heliopolis would now have hardly recognised their doctrines in the exalted faith of the Aton, though here and there some point of close contact might have been observed. One may also detect slight resemblances to the Adonis religions of Syria, from whence the Aton had originally come. Mention has already been made of the worship of Adonis. So widespread was that deity's power that it very naturally affected many other religions. In the Biblical Psalms one finds several echoes of this old pagan worship, as for example in the lines from Psalm xix., which read :—

> The heavens declare the glory of God. . . .
> In them hath he set à tabernacle for the sun,
> Which is a bridegroom coming out of his chamber,
> And he rejoiceth as a strong man to run a race.
> There is nothing hid from the heat thereof.

Here one surely must recognise the youthful Adonis, the bridegroom of Venus. And similarly in the Heliopolitan worship, at the commencement of Akhnaton's reign, the sun, Ra, is referred to in the following terms : "Thou art beautiful and youthful as Aton before thy mother Hathor [Venus]."

In Akhnaton's religion one may still catch a fleeting glimpse of Adonis.   One of the king's courtiers, named May, held the office of "Overseer of the House for sending Aton to rest." [1] Akhnaton's queen is mentioned in the tomb of Ay under the peculiar title of "She who sends the Aton to rest with a sweet voice, and with her two beautiful hands bearing two systrums." This "house" was, no doubt, the temple at which the vesper prayers to the Aton were said at sunset, and from the above title of the queen it would seem that she had particular charge of these evening ceremonies.   One cannot contemplate the fact that it was a woman who officiated at a ceremony which consisted of a lament [2] for the death of the sun without seeing in it some connection, however faint, with the story of Venus and Adonis.   The lament of Venus for the death of Adonis—*i.e.*, the setting of the sun

---

[1] So Prof. Breasted translates the Egyptian *sehetep*, though it would be possible to give it other interpretations.

[2] Cf. such expressions as "When thou settest they die," and others used in Akhnaton's hymns.

—was one of the fundamental ceremonies of the
Mediterranean religions. Here again was a connection with an older religion for Akhnaton to
consider and perhaps to purge away; and one
may suppose that all such derivatives from
earlier faiths were gradually eliminated as the
young king developed his creed. Soon not a
scrap of superstition remained in the religion;
and one may credit this Pharaoh of three thousand
years ago with as great a freedom from the
trammels of traditional superstition as that of
the advanced thinker of to-day.

7. THE SPIRITUAL NEEDS OF THE SOUL
AFTER DEATH.

"Truly the light is sweet, and a pleasant thing
it is for the eyes to behold the sun," says Holy
Writ in words which might have fallen from
the lips of Akhnaton; "but though a man live
many years and rejoice in them all, yet let him
remember the days of darkness, for they shall
be many." As Akhnaton had completely rev-
olutionised the beliefs of the Egyptians as to

the nature of God, so he altered and purged their theories regarding the existence of the soul after death. According to the old beliefs, as we have seen, the soul of a man had to pass through awful places up to the judgment throne of Osiris, where he was weighed in the balances. If he was found wanting he was devoured by a ferocious monster, but if the scales turned in his favour he was accepted into the Elysian fields. So many were the spirits, bogies, and demigods which he was likely to meet before the goal was reached that he had to know by heart a tedious string of formulæ, the correct repetition of which, and the correct making of the related magic, alone ensured his safe passage.

Akhnaton flung all these formulæ into the fire. Djins, bogies, spirits, monsters, demigods, demons, and Osiris himself with all his court, were swept into the blaze and reduced to ashes. Akhnaton believed that when a man died his soul continued to exist as a kind of astral, immaterial ghost, sometimes resting in the dreamy halls of heaven, and sometimes visiting, in shadowy form, the haunts of the earthly

life. By some of the inscriptions one is led to
suppose that, as in the fourth article of the
Christian faith, so in the teachings of Akhnaton,
the body was thought to take again after death
its "flesh, bones, and all things appertaining to
the perfection of man's nature." But just as
there is some doubt and some vagueness in the
mind of Christian thinkers as to the meaning
of this article, so in Akhnaton's doctrine there
was some uncertainty as to whether the body
was entirely spiritual or in a manner material
in its hazy existence in the Hills of the West.
The disembodied soul still craved the pleasures
of earthly life and shunned its sorrows; still felt
hunger and thirst and enjoyed a draught of water
or a meal of solid food; still warmed itself in
the sunshine or sought coolness in the shadows.

We hear nothing of hell; for Akhnaton, in the
tenderness of his heart, could not bring himself
to believe that God would allow suffering in
any of His creatures, however sinful. The inscriptions seem rather to indicate that there was
no future life for the wicked,—that they were
annihilated; though in almost every man one
may suppose that there was enough good to

recommend him to the mercy of a God so loving as the Aton.

The first great wish of the deceased was that he might each day leave the dim underworld in order to see the light of the sun upon earth. This had been the prayer of the Egyptians from time immemorial, and to suit the religion of the Aton its wording alone was changed. The disciple of Akhnaton asked to be allowed "to go out from the underworld in the morning to see Aton as he rises." He prayed insistently, passionately, in varied language, that his spirit might "go forth to see the sun's rays," that his "two eyes might be opened to see the sun," that there might be "no failure to see it," that the "vision of the sun's fair face might never be lost to him," that he "might obtain a sight of the beauty of each recurring sunrise," and that "the sun's rays might spread over his body." Sometimes it is the Aton whom the soul thus craves to see; sometimes it is Ra, the sun; but always it seems to be the actual light and warmth of the sunshine which is so passionately desired. The abstract conditions of the future life could but be interpreted in terms of human experience; and in contemplating that cold, desolate mystery of death, Akhnaton could find no better means of banishing the gloom than by praying for a continuance of the blessed light of the day. And the man who prayed that his soul might see the sunshine but asked that he might still know the joy of the presence of God, for God was the light of the world.

His second wish was that he might retain the favour of the king and queen after death, and that his soul might serve their souls in the palaces of the dead. He asks for "readiness in the presence of the King" to do his bidding; he prays that he may be admitted into the palace, "entering it in favour and leaving it in love"; that he may "attend the King every day"; and that he may "receive honour in the presence of the King."

For his mental contentment in the underworld he earnestly desired that "his name might be remembered and established on earth," that there might be "a happy memory of him in the King's palace," and "a continuance of his name in the mouths of the courtiers," where he hoped that it "might be welcome." "May my name thrive in the tomb-chapel," he says.   "May my name not be to seek in my mansion.   May it be celebrated for ever."   So, too, at the present day the words *In Memoriam* are goodly words; and that a man's memory may be kept green is a thing very generally desired.

8. THE MATERIAL NEEDS OF THE SOUL.

In order that the soul might have its link with earth, the worshipper of the Aton prayed that his mummy might remain "firm" and uncorrupted, that the "flesh might live upon the bones," and that his limbs might remain "knit together."   The Egyptians of other days believed that the body itself would live again at the resurrection, this being the reason why they attempted so carefully to preserve it; and Akhnaton does not appear to have altered this conception of the nature of the material body.   So, too, in the Christian faith it is thought that at the last day the graves will give up their dead.

The spiritual body retained the form and the individuality of the material body, and therefore, in a somewhat vague manner, it was thought that the needs of the soul would not be very dissimilar from those of the body upon earth. Christ, after His resurrection, asked for food; and the feasts of Paradise are more than allegory to many a Christian. Likewise the follower of Akhnaton believed that material food, or its spiritual equivalent, would be necessary to the soul's welfare in the next world. "Mày I be called by my name," says he, "and come at the summons, in order to feed upon the good things provided upon the temple altar." It would seem that through fidelity to the Aton creed he might have the privilege of partaking of the offerings made at the great ceremonies in the temple; for, after these sacrifices had been offered, the food, probably, was distributed to the priests and to those attached to the tombs, who represented the interests of the dead. Thus the deceased prays that he may enjoy "a reception of that which has been offered in the temple"; "a reception of offerings of the King's giving in every shrine"; "a drink-offering in the temple of Aton"; "food deposited on the altar every day"; and "everything that is offered in the

sanctuary of Aton in the City of the Horizon of
Aton." He further asks that "wine may be
poured out" for him, and that "the children of
his house may spill a libation for him at the
entrance of his tomb."

While life lasted God was very apparent to
those who sought Him. Wherever the sun
shone, wherever the great pulse of the earth
beat beneath one, wherever the river flowed or
the garden bloomed, there was God to be found;
for God was happiness, was beauty, was love.
But when the cold mists of death had enveloped
a man, when there was no longer any spring-time
nor any opening of the blossoms, how should
there be contentment any more? From the
depths of his heart Akhnaton urged his followers
to pray God that He might provide this happiness, though it could only be voiced in very
human words. It was not "sweet perfume" nor
"the smell of incense" that the soul required;
but how else could the pleasure of light-hearted-
ness be worded? They prayed that their "limbs
might be provided with pleasure every day." In
the stagnant air of the tomb they craved for the
touch of the "sweet breeze," for "the breath of

K

the pleasant airs of the north wind." They hoped
in shadowy form to be able to visit the beloved
scenes of their lifetime. "May I raise myself up
and forget languor," prays one. "May I leave
and enter my mansion," says another. "May my
soul not be shut off from that which it desires.
May I walk as I will in the grove that I have
made upon earth. May I drink the water at
the edge of my lake every day without ceasing."
"May water be poured out from my cistern,"
cries a third; "may I receive fruit from my
trees." Incessantly each man implores God to
grant that he may cool his parched lips with
water. "A draught of water at the banks of
the river," is his desire; "a draught of water at
the swirl of the stream." While he smells "the
scent of the wind" blowing amidst the petals
of "a bouquet of Aton," and while there runs "a
brook of water" by his side, he need not know
the horror of death. And thus, by receiving
"everything good and sweet," he may hope for
"health and prosperity" in the hills and the
valleys of the West; for a "happy life, provided
with pleasure and joy," for "amusement, merri-
ment, and delight," and for a "daily rejoicing"
throughout eternity.

It may be argued that this material conception of the life after death is not equal in purity of tone to the faith of the Aton. But is it, then, less lofty to believe in a heaven in which there is joy and laughter, a scent of flowers, and a breath of north wind, than in one where the streets are paved with gold, and where there are many mansions? By no religion in the world is Christianity so closely approached as by the faith of Akhnaton; and if the Pharaoh's doctrines as to immortality are not altogether convincing, neither are the Christian doctrines, as they are now interpreted, altogether without fault. In the above pages it has been necessary always to compare Akhnaton's creed with Christianity, since there is so much common to the two religions; but it should be remembered that this comparison must of necessity be unfavourable to the Pharaoh's doctrine, revealing as it does its shortcomings. Let the reader remember that Akhnaton lived some thirteen hundred years before the birth of Christ, at an age when the world was steeped in superstition and sunk in the fogs of idolatry. Bearing this in mind, he will not fail to see in that tenderly loving Father whom the boy-Pharaoh worshipped an early revelation of the God to whom we of the present day bow down; and once more he will find how true are the words—

"God fulfils Himself in many ways."

Since writing the above, another point in Akhnaton's teaching has become apparent, from the scenes, recently discovered by the present writer, in the tomb of Rames. There is a scene often represented upon the walls of tombs of Dynasty XVIII. which seems to represent human sacrifice. The figure of a man is seen dragged to the tomb upon a sledge, and Sir Gaston Maspero has pointed out that this can hardly be anything else than such a sacrifice. This scene was shown on one of the walls of the tomb of Rames, and evidently dated from a period previous to Akhnaton's revolution. When, however, the young king had formulated his religion of love he could not tolerate a barbaric and cruel ceremony of this kind. We thus find that the entire scene is here obliterated, almost certainly by the king's agents. The objection to human sacrifice is closely in accord with his objection to human suffering as recorded on page 175.

V.

THE TENTH TO THE TWELFTH YEARS OF THE REIGN OF AKHNATON.

"One must be moved with involuntary admiration for the young king who in such an age found such thoughts in his heart."—BREASTED: 'History of Egypt.'

1. THE HYMNS OF THE ATON WORSHIPPERS.

IN the tombs of rich persons who had lived and died previous to the time of Akhnaton, a large portion of the walls had been covered with religious inscriptions; and when at first the nobles of the City of the Horizon of Aton were planning their sepulchres they must have been at a loss to know what to substitute for these forbidden formulæ. Soon, however, it became the custom to write there short extracts from the hymns which were sung in the temples of the Aton. In a few cases

these inscriptions supply us with a definite
psalm which, although short, seems to be
complete. In one tomb—that of Ay—however,
there is a copy of a much more elaborate
hymn; and it would thus seem that there
were two main psalms in use in the temples,
a longer and a shorter version of the same
composition.

It was not unusual for the Egyptians to
compose hymns in honour of their gods, and
a few such have been preserved to us upon
the walls of the old temples. Like the Hebrew
psalms of later date, they are not always of a
very high moral tone. They are often but
chants of victory, dealing in battles, in
thunders, and in tempests, and glorying in
the wrath of heaven. The longer hymn to
the Aton, which is here given in full, is quite
unlike any of these compositions, and both in
purity of tone and in beauty of style it must
rank high amongst the poems of antiquity.

[1] " Thy dawning is beautiful in the horizon of heaven,
O living Aton, Beginning of life!
When Thou risest in the eastern horizon of heaven,

---

[1] Professor Breasted's translation.

Thou fillest every land with Thy beauty;
For Thou are beautiful, great, glittering, high over the earth;
Thy rays, they encompass the lands, even all Thou hast made.
Thou art Ra, and Thou hast carried them all away captive;
Thou bindest them by Thy love.
Though Thou art afar, Thy rays are on earth;
Though Thou art on high, Thy footprints are the day.

When Thou settest in the western horizon of heaven,
The world is in darkness like the dead.
Men sleep in their chambers,
Their heads are wrapped up,
Their nostrils stopped, and none seeth the other.
Stolen are all their things that are under their heads,
While they know it not.
Every lion cometh forth from his den,
All serpents, they sting.
Darkness reigns,
The world is in silence:
He that made them has gone to rest in His horizon.

Bright is the earth, when Thou risest in the horizon,
When Thou shinest as Aton by day.
The darkness is banished
When Thou sendest forth Thy rays;
The two lands [of Egypt] are in daily festivity,
Awake and standing upon their feet,
For Thou hast raised them up.
Their limbs bathed, they take their clothing,
Their arms uplifted in adoration to Thy dawning.
Then in all the world they do their work.

All cattle rest upon the herbage,
All trees and plants flourish;
The birds flutter in their marshes,
Their wings uplifted in adoration to Thee.

All the sheep dance upon their feet,
All winged things fly,
They live when Thou hast shone upon them.

The barques sail up-stream and down-stream alike.
Every highway is open because Thou hast dawned.
The fish in the river leap up before Thee,
And Thy rays are in the midst of the great sea.

Thou art He who createst the man-child in woman,
Who makest seed in man,
Who giveth life to the son in the body of his mother,
Who soothest him that he may not weep,
A nurse [even] in the womb.
Who giveth breath to animate every one that He maketh.
When he cometh forth from the body . . .
On the day of his birth,
Thou openest his mouth in speech,
Thou suppliest his necessities.

When the chicken crieth in the egg-shell,
Thou givest him breath therein, to preserve him alive ;
When Thou hast perfected him
That he may pierce the egg,
He cometh forth from the egg,
To chirp with all his might ;
He runneth about upon his two feet,
When he hath come forth therefrom.

How manifold are all Thy works !
They are hidden from before us,
O Thou sole God, whose powers no other possesseth.
Thou didst create the earth according to Thy desire,
While Thou wast alone :
Men, all cattle large and small,
All that are upon the earth,

That go about upon their feet ;
All that are on high,
That fly with their wings.
The countries of Syria and Nubia
The land of Egypt ;
Thou settest every man in his place
Thou suppliest their necessities.
Every one has his possessions,
And his days are reckoned.
Their tongues are divers in speech,
Their forms likewise and their skins,
For Thou, divider, hast divided the peoples.

Thou makest the Nile in the nether world,
Thou bringest it at Thy desire, to preserve the people alive.
O Lord of them all, when feebleness is in them,
O Lord of every house, who risest for them,
O sun of day, the fear of every distant land,
Thou makest [also] their life.
Thou hast set a Nile in heaven,
That it may fall for them,
Making floods upon the mountains, like the great sea,
And watering their fields among their towns.

How excellent are Thy designs, O Lord of eternity !
The Nile in heaven is for the strangers,
And for the cattle of every land that go upon their feet ;
But the Nile, it cometh from the nether world for Egypt.
Thus Thy rays nourish every garden ;
When Thou risest they live, and grow by Thee.

Thou makest the seasons, in order to create all Thy works ;
Winter bringeth them coolness,
And the heat [the summer bringeth].
Thou hast made the distant heaven in order to rise therein,
In order to behold all that Thou didst make,

While Thou wast alone,
Rising in Thy form as Living Aton,
Dawning, shining afar off, and returning.

Thou makest the beauty of form through Thyself alone,
Cities, towns, and settlements,
On highway or on river,
All eyes see Thee before them,
For Thou art Aton of the day over the earth.

Thou art in my heart;
There is no other that knoweth Thee,
Save Thy son Akhnaton.
Thou hast made him wise in Thy designs
And in Thy might.
The world is in Thy hand,
Even as Thou hast made them.
When Thou hast risen they live;
When Thou settest they die.
For Thou art duration, beyond mere limbs;
By Thee man liveth,
And their eyes look upon Thy beauty
Until Thou settest.
All labour is laid aside
When Thou settest in the west.
When Thou risest they are made to grow. . . .
Since Thou didst establish the earth,
Thou hast raised them up for Thy son,
Who came forth from Thy limbs,
The King, living in truth, . . .
Akhnaton, whose life is long;
[And for] the great royal wife, his beloved,
Mistress of the Two Lands, . . . Nefertiti,
Living and flourishing for ever and ever."

2. THE SIMILARITY OF AKHNATON'S HYMN
TO PSALM CIV.

In reading this truly beautiful hymn one cannot fail to be struck by its similarity to Psalm civ. A parallel will show this most clearly :—

AKHNATON'S HYMN.

The world is in darkness like the dead. Every lion cometh forth from his den ; all serpents sting. Darkness reigns.

When Thou risest in the horizon . . . the darkness is banished. . . . Then in all the world they do their work.

All trees and plants flourish, . . . the birds flutter in their marshes. . . . All sheep dance upon their feet.

The ships sail up-stream and down-stream alike. . . . The fish in the river leap up before Thee ; and Thy rays are in the midst of the great sea.

How manifold are all Thy works ! . . . Thou didst create

PSALM CIV.

Thou makest the darkness and it is night, wherein all the beasts of the forest do creep forth. The young lions roar after their prey ; they seek their meat from God.

The sun riseth, they get them away, and lay them down in their dens. Man goeth forth unto his work, and to his labour until the evening.

The trees of the Lord are full of sap, . . . wherein the birds make their nests. . . . The high hills are a refuge for the wild goats.

Yonder is the sea, great and wide, wherein are . . . both small and great beasts. There go the ships. . . .

O Lord, how manifold are Thy works ! In wisdom hast

the earth according to Thy desire,—men, all cattle, . . . all that are upon the earth. . . .

Thou made them all. The earth is full of Thy creatures.

Thou hast set a Nile in heaven that it may fall for them, making floods upon the mountains . . . and watering their fields. The Nile in heaven is for the service of the strangers, and for the cattle of every land.

He watereth the hills from above : the earth is filled with the fruit of Thy works. He bringeth forth grass for the cattle, and green herb for the service of men.

Thou makest the seasons. . . . Thou hast made the distant heaven in order to rise therein, . . . dawning, shining afar off, and returning.

He appointed the moon for certain seasons, and the sun knoweth his going down.

The world is in Thy hand, even as Thou hast made them. When thou hast risen they live; when Thou settest they die. . . . By Thee man liveth.

These wait all upon Thee. . . . When Thou givest them [food] they gather it ; and when Thou openest Thy hand they are filled with good. When Thou hidest Thy face they are troubled : when Thou takest away their breath they die.

In face of this remarkable similarity one can hardly doubt that there is a direct connection between the two compositions ; and it becomes necessary to ask whether both Akhnaton's hymn and this Hebrew psalm were derived from a common Syrian source, or whether Psalm civ. is derived from this Pharaoh's original poem. Both views are admissible ; but in consideration of

An Example of the Friendly Relations between Syria and Egypt.

A Syrian soldier named Terura, and his wife, Aariburæ, attended by an Egyptian servant, who assists him to hold the tube through which he is drinking wine from a jar. From a tablet found at El Amarna. (Zeit. Aeg. Spr. xxxvi. 126.)

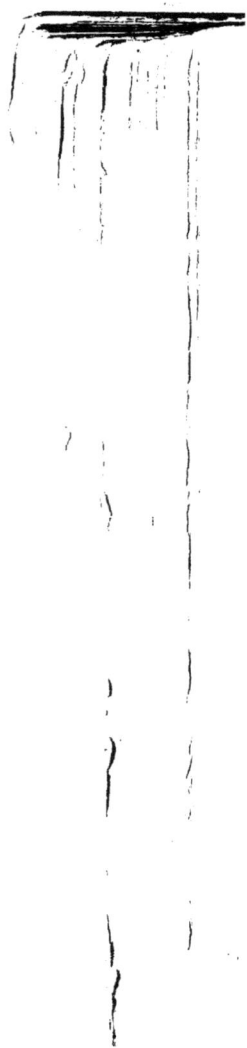

Akhnaton's peculiar ability and originality there seems considerable likelihood that he is the author in the first instance of this gem of the Psalter.

When the young Pharaoh composed this hymn he was probably neither much more nor less than twenty or twenty-one years of age,—a period of life at which many of the world's greatest poets have written some of their fairest poems. One sees that he believed himself to be the only man to whom God had revealed Himself; and the fact that he never admits that he was in any way taught to regard God as he did, but always speaks of himself, and is spoken of, as the originator and teacher of the faith, indicates that the ideas expressed in the hymn were entirely his own.

3. MERYRA IS MADE HIGH PRIEST OF ATON.

The religion of the Aton had now assumed shape and symmetry, and had been firmly established in the new capital as the creed of the court. Akhnaton was thus able to intrust its administration and organisation there to one of his nobles

who had hearkened to his teaching, and to turn
his attention to other affairs, and more especially
to the conversion of the rest of Egypt. As head
of the state a thousand matters daily claimed
his consideration, and his high principles led
him to stray further along the by-paths of
administration than had been the wont of the
Pharaohs before him. His ill-health did not
permit him to tax his brain with impunity, and
yet there was never a king of Egypt before or
after him whose mind was so fruitful of thoughts
and of schemes. The young king himself ex-
pounded to his followers the doctrines which he
wished them to embrace, and one may suppose
that he sat for many an hour in the halls of
his palace, or under the trees in the gardens
beside the Nile, earnestly telling of the beauties
of the Aton to officials and nobles.

No one had accepted the king's teaching with
greater readiness than a certain Meryra, who
seens to have early associated himself with the
movement; and it was to him that Akhnaton
now handed over the office of " High Priest of
the Aton in the City of the Horizon of Aton,"
in order to free himself for the great task of

administering his kingdom and converting it to
his way of thinking. Unfortunately we know
very little of the career of Meryra, but on the
walls of his tomb in the hills behind the capital
there are a few reliefs which may here be
described as illustrating events in his life and
in the life of Akhnaton.

One of these scenes shows us the investiture
of Meryra as High Priest. The king is seen
with his wife and one of his daughters standing
at a window of the gaily decorated *loggia* of
the palace. The sill of the window is massed
with bright - coloured cushions, and over these
the royal personages lean forward to address
Meryra and the company assembled in the
pillared gallery outside. The outer surface of
the *loggia* wall is brightly ornamented either
with real or painted garlands of lotus - flowers,
and with the many-coloured patterns usual upon
such buildings in ancient Egypt. Ribbons, fluttering in the breeze, hang from the delicate lotus-
pillars which support the roof, and vie in brilliancy
with the red and blue ostrich-plume fans and
standards carried by the officials.

Leaning from the window, with arm outstretched, Akhnaton bids Meryra rise from his knees, on to which he had cast himself on reaching the royal presence. Then solemnly the king addresses his favoured disciple in the following words :—" Behold, I make thee High Priest of the Aton for me in the Temple of the Aton in the City of the Horizon of Aton. I do this for love of thee, and I say unto thee : O my servant who hearkenest to the teaching, my heart is satisfied with everything which thou hast done. I give thee this office, and I say unto thee : thou shalt eat the food of Pharaoh, thy lord, in the Temple of Aton."

Immediately the assembled company crowd round Meryra and lift him shoulder - high, while the new High Priest cries, "Abundant are the rewards which the Aton knows to give when his heart is pleased." The king then presents Meryra with the insignia of his office, and with various costly gifts, which are taken charge of by the servants and attendants who stand outside the gallery. Behind these attendants, at the outskirts of the scene, one observes the chariot which is to convey the High Priest back to his villa ; fan-bearers who shall

run before and behind him; women of the
household who shall beat upon tambourines at
the head of the procession, and who already
dance with excitement as they see Meryra
hoisted on to his friend's shoulder; and still
other women who shall make the roadway rich
with flowers.

This is no solemn and occult initiation of an
ascetic into the mystery of the new religion,
but rather the elevation of a good fellow to a
popular post of honour. There was no mystery
in the faith of the Aton. Frankness, openness,
and sincerity were the dominant themes of
Akhnaton's teaching,—a worship of God in the
blessed light of the day, the singing of merry
psalms in the open courts of the temple; and
the chosen High Priest was more likely to have
been a deep-thinking, clean-lived, honest-hearted,
God-fearing, family man, than an ascetic who
had abandoned the pomps and the vanities of
this world. The point at which Akhnaton's
religion differs most widely from Christianity
is here to be observed: the Pharaoh, while en-
couraging the Simple Life, did not preach the
mortification of the flesh, but only the control

of the body. The comforts of life, the brilliancy
of decoration, the charms of music, the beauties
of painting and sculpture, the pleasure of good
company, the tonic of a bowl of wine, were all
as acceptable to him, in moderation, as to the
Preacher in Ecclesiastes.

4. THE ROYAL FAMILY VISIT THE TEMPLE.

When Meryra had been installed, the king
and royal family made a formal visit to the
temple at the time of sunset, and this is likewise represented in the High Priest's tomb. For
the first time in the history of Egypt one is
permitted to see the Pharaoh as he drove
through the streets of the capital in his chariot.
No king before Akhnaton had allowed an artist
to represent him in aught but celestial poses;
but out of his love for truth and reality
Akhnaton had dispensed with this convention,
and encouraged the regarding of himself as a
mortal man. On this occasion we see him standing in his gorgeously decorated chariot, reins
and whip in hand, himself driving the two

spirited horses, the coloured ostrich plumes on whose heads nod and toss as the superb animals prance along. The queen, also driving her own chariot, follows close behind; and after her again come the princesses, heading a noble group of chariots belonging to the court officials and ladies - in - waiting, these being driven by charioteers. The shining harness, the dancing red and blue plumes of the horses, the many-coloured robes, the feathered standards of the nobles, the fluttering ribbons, all go to make the cavalcade a sight to bring the townspeople running from their houses. A guard of soldiers, armed with spears, shields, battle - axes, bows, and clubs, races along on foot in front of the royal party to clear the road. Here, besides Egyptians, are bearded Asiatics from the king's Syrian dominions, befeathered negroes from the Mazoi tribes of Nubia, and Libyans from the west, wearing the plaited side-lock of hair hanging from their heads.

The party is seen to be nearing the temple, and Meryra stands before the gateway ready to greet his lord. Four men kneel near him holding aloft the coloured ostrich-plume fans, which

will be wafted to and fro above the king's head
when he has alighted from his chariot; and
others kneel, lifting their hands in reverent
salutation.   Great bulls, fattened like the prize
cattle of modern times, are led forth, garlands
of flowers thrown around their huge necks, and
bouquets of flowers fastened between their horns.
These are attended by grooms, also bearing
bunches of flowers.   Two groups of female musicians, clad in flowing robes, wave their arms and
beat upon tambourines.

The temple, which will be described later, is
this day garlanded with flowers, and every altar
is heaped high with offerings.   Now the king
has entered the building, and a further scene
shows the royal family worshipping at the high
altar, which is piled up with offerings of joints
of meat, geese, vegetables, fruit, and flowers,
surmounted by bronze bowls filled with burning
oil.   Akhnaton and Nefertiti stand before the
altar, each with the right arm raised in the act
of sprinkling the fragrant gums of Araby upon
the flames.   The upper part of the king's body
is bare, but from his waist depends a graceful

skirt of fine linen, ornamented with sash - like ribbons of a red material, which flutter about his bare legs. The queen's robe covers the whole of her body, but is so transparent that one can see her fair form with almost the distinctness of nudity. A red sash is bound round her waist, and the two ends fall almost to the ground. Neither of the two wears any jewels; and the simplicity of the soft, flowing robes, with their bright-red sashes, is extremely marked. Two little princesses stand behind the king and queen, each shaking from a systrum a note of praise to God. Meryra, accompanied by an assistant, stands bowing before the king, and near by another priest burns some sweet - smelling incense. Not far away there sits a group of eight blind musicians, — fat elderly men, who clap their hands and sing to the accompaniment of a seven-stringed harp, giving praise to the sunlight which they cannot see, but yet can feel as "the heat which is in Aton" penetrates into their bones.

In still another series of reliefs we are shown a scene representing the reward of Meryra by

Akhnaton on some occasion when he had been
particularly successful in collecting the yearly
dues of the temple from the estates on the opposite bank of the river.   The ceremony took
place in the granary buildings at the edge of
the water.   One sees a group of boats moored
at the quay, and on the shore are several cattle-
pens filled with lowing cattle.   The granaries
are stored with all manner of good things, and
Meryra stands triumphant in front of them as
the king addresses him.

" Let the Superintendent of the Treasury of
the Jewels take Meryra," says Akhnaton, "and
hang gold on his neck at the front, and gold
on his feet, because of his obedience to the
teaching of Pharaoh ;" and immediately the attendants literally heap the gold collars and
necklaces one above the other upon the High
Priest's neck. Scribes write down a rapid sum-
mary of the events; the attendants and fan-
bearers bow low; and Meryra is conducted back
to his village with music and with dancing, while
Akhnaton returns to his palace, and, no doubt,
sinks exhausted on to his cushions.

5. AKHNATON IN HIS PALACE.

The reliefs and paintings upon the tombs often show the Pharaoh reclining thus, in a languid manner, as though the duties of his high calling had sapped all the strength from him. Never before had a Pharaoh been represented to his subjects in such human attitudes. The privacy of the palace is penetrated in these scenes, and we see the king, who loved to teach his followers the beauty of family life, in the midst of his own family. One or two of these representations must here be described. In one instance the royal family is shown inside a beautiful pavilion, the roof of which is supported by wooden pillars painted with many colours and having capitals carved in high relief to represent wild geese suspended by their legs, and above them bunches of flowers : just such a grouping as one might see in some sporting house of the present day. The pillars are hung with garlands of flowers, and from the ceiling there droop festoons of flowers and trailing branches of vines. The roof of the pavilion on the outside is edged by an endless line of gleaming cobras, probably wrought in bronze.

Inside this fair arbor stand a group of naked girls playing upon the harp, the lute, and the lyre, and, no doubt, singing to that accompaniment the artless love-songs of the period. Servants are shown attending to the jars of wine which stand at the side of the enclosure. The king is seen leaning back upon the cushions of an arm-chair, as though tired out and sick at heart.   In the fingers of his left hand he idly dandles a few flowers, while with his right hand he languidly holds out a delicate bowl in order that the wine in it may be replenished. This is done by the queen, who is standing before him, all solicitous for his comfort. She pours the wine from a vessel, causing it to pass through a strainer before flowing into the bowl. Three little princesses stand near by : one of them laden with bouquets of flowers, another holding out some sweetmeat upon a dish, and a third talking to her father.

In another scene the king and queen are both shown seated upon comfortable chairs, while a servant waits upon them. The king is eating

a roasted pigeon, holding it in his fingers; and
Nefertiti is represented drinking from a prettily
shaped cup. The light, transparent robes which
they wear indicate that this is the midday
meal; but unfortunately the painting is so much
damaged that nothing but the royal figures
remains.

6. HISTORICAL EVENTS OF THIS PERIOD OF AKHNATON'S REIGN.

There is very little historical information to
be procured for these years of the king's reign.
When he had been about ten or eleven years
upon the throne, and was some twenty-one years
of age, his fourth daughter, Nefernefernaton, was
born. The queen had presented no son to
Akhnaton to succeed him, but he does not seem
in this emergency to have cared to turn to any
secondary wives; and, as far as we can tell, he
remained all his life a monogamist, although
this was in direct opposition to all traditional
custom. Steadily during these years the king's
health seems to have grown more precarious,

for almost daily he must have overtaxed his
strength.   His brain was so active that he could
not submit to be idle; and even when he re-
clined amidst the flowers in his' garden, his
whole soul was straining upwards in the attempt
to pierce the barrier which lay between him and
the God who had caused those flowers to bloom.
The maturity of his creed at this period leads
one to suppose that he had given to it his very
life's force; and when it is remembered that
at the same time his attention was occupied by
the administration of a kingdom which he had
twisted out of all semblance to its former shape,
the wonder is that his brain was at all able to
stand the incessant strain.   Rare indeed must
have been those idle moments which the artists of
the City of the Horizon attempted to represent.

In the twelfth year of his reign, the tribute
of the vassal kingdoms reached such a high
value that a particular record was made of it,
and scenes showing its reception were sculptured
in the tombs of Huya and Meryra II.[1]   An in-

---

[1] In the tomb of Huya the scene is dated in the twelfth year, as
here recorded, and there are four daughters shown, which is the
number one is led by other evidence to suppose were then alive.
The scene in the tomb of Meryra II. has precisely the same date,

scription beside the scene in the tomb of Huya
reads thus :—

> Year twelve, the second month of winter, the
> eighth day. . . . The King . . . and the Queen
> . . . living for ever and ever, made a public
> appearance on the great palanquin of gold, to re-
> ceive the tribute of Syria and Ethiopia, and of
> the west and the east. All the countries were
> collected at one time, and also the islands in
> the midst of the sea ; bringing offerings to the
> King when he was on the great throne of the
> City of the Horizon of Aton, in order to receive
> the imposts of every land and granting them [in
> return] the breath of life.

The king and queen are shown seated in the
state palanquin side by side ; and although

but six daughters are shown, and there is evidence to show that that
number is not to be looked for previous to the fifteenth year of the
reign, the first daughter being born in about the fifth year, the
second in the seventh, the third in the ninth, the fourth in the
eleventh, the fifth in the thirteenth, and the sixth in the fifteenth
year, in all probability. Thus the scene in Meryra II. may perhaps
represent no particular reception of the tribute of any one year, but
the artist may have had in mind the great tribute of the twelfth
year while representing the occurrence in the fifteenth or sixteenth
year, at which date his work was taking place. Or again the date in
this latter tomb may be a misreading or miswriting. The scene described above is that represented in the tomb of Meryra, as it is
more elaborate than the other ; but the inscription is that found in
the tomb of Huya.

Akhnaton holds the insignia of royalty, and is evidently very much upon his dignity, the queen's arm has found its way around his waist, and there lovingly rests for all the world to see. The palanquin, probably made of wood entirely covered with gold foil, is a very imposing structure : a large double throne, borne aloft by stout poles upon the shoulders of the court officials. The arm-rests are carved in the form of sphinxes, which rise above a glistening hedge of cobras, and the throne is flanked on either side by the figure of a lion carved in the round. A priest walks in front of the palanquin sending up a cloud of incense from a censer, and professional mummers dance and skip in the roadway in advance of the procession. Behind the royal couple walk the princesses, attended by their nurses and ladies ; and on all sides are arrayed courtiers, officers, soldiers, and servants.

Soon the ground marked out for the ceremony is reached, and the king and queen betake themselves to a gorgeous little pavilion which has been erected for them, and here they sit together upon a double throne, their feet supported upon hassocks. The queen sits upon Akhnaton's left, and in the picture her figure is hidden by that of her husband; but as her right arm is seen to encircle his waist, and her left hand to hold his left hand, one may suppose that she is reclining against him, with her royal head upon his shoulder. Nefertiti was the mother of a family of children, but was not more than about twenty[1] years of age; and as she is said to have been extremely beautiful, one may presume that this scene of conjugal affection was not without its -charm. The little princesses cluster round the throne, one of them holding a young gazelle in her arms, while another strokes its head.

In front of this pavilion the deputations from the vassal kingdoms pass by; and in order that the king may not be wearied by their ceremonious homage, a group of professional wrestlers, boxers, and fencers is provided for his diversion; while near them some buffoons and mummers dance and tumble to the accompaniment of castanets and hand - clapping. The tribute of

[1] Her first child, it will be remembered, was born when she was about thirteen.

Syria is brought by long-robed Asiatics, who cast themselves upon their knees before the throne with hands uplifted in salutation. Splendid Syrian horses are led past, and behind them chariots are wheeled or carried along. Then come groups of slaves, handcuffed, but not cruelly bound nor maltreated, as was the custom under other Pharaohs. Bows, spears, shields, daggers, elephant-tusks, and other objects, are carried past and deposited upon the ground near the pavilion; while beautiful vases of precious metal or costly stone are held aloft for the king to admire. Wild animals are led across the ground by their keepers, and amongst these a tame mountain lion must have caused something of a sensation. Several nude girls, selected probably for their beauty, walk past; and one may suppose that they will find subsequent employment amongst the handmaidens in the palace.

From the "islands in the midst of the sea" come beautiful vases, some ornamented with figures in the round. From Libya ostrich eggs and ostrich feathers are brought. The tribute of Nubia and the Sudan is carried past by

befeathered negroes, and consists mainly of bars
and rings of gold and bags of gold-dust, procured from the mines in the Eastern Desert.
Shields, weapons, tusks, and skins are also to
be seen, and cattle and antelopes are led before
the throne. As the Asiatics had startled the
assembly by bringing with them a lion, so
the negroes cause a stir by leading forward
a panther of large size. Finally, male and
female slaves, the latter carrying their babies
in baskets upon their backs, are marched past
the pavilion; but here again these slaves are
not maltreated. It is particularly noticeable
that the groups of miserable captives which one
sees in all such scenes of other periods, with
their arms bound in agonising positions and
their knees giving way under them, are entirely
absent from the representations of Akhnaton's
ceremonies. Human suffering was a thing hateful to the young Pharaoh who knew so well
the meaning of physical distress; and the tor-
tures of the prisoners, or the beheading of some
rebel, such as would have been a feature of an
occasion of this kind under Amonhotep II., or
even, perhaps, under Amonhotep III., would

have been as revolting to Akhnaton as it would be to us.

7. QUEEN TIY VISITS THE CITY OF THE HORIZON.

Akhnaton had left Thebes, as we have seen, in about the eighth year of his reign; but his mother, Queen Tiy, seems to have been unwilling to accompany him, and to have decided to remain in her palace at the foot of the Theban hills. It is probable that she had not encouraged her son to create the new capital, and the removal of the court from Thebes must have been something of a grief to her, though no doubt she recognised the necessity of the step. In spite of advancing years she must have sorely missed the pomp and circumstance of the splendid court over which she had once presided. Up to the fourth year of her son's reign she had been dominant, and the whole known world had bowed the knee to her. The luxuries of the many kingdoms over which she held sway had been hers to enjoy; but now, with the king and the nobles gone to the City of the Horizon, and every penny which could be collected gone with them, the old queen must have been obliged to live a quiet, retired life in a palace which was probably falling into rapid ruin.   Her little daughter, Baketaton, appears to have lived with her; and it may be that some of her other daughters were still with her, though of them we hear nothing, and it is more probable that they had already died.   It seems likely that she paid occasional state visits to her son, and permanent accommodation was provided for her in the City of the Horizon should she at any time desire to stay there.   Her major-domo, an elderly man named Huya, appears to have lived for part of the year at the new capital, where a tomb was made for him; and it is from the reliefs on the walls of this tomb that we obtain the knowledge of one of these state visits made by the old queen to Akhnaton.   There is no evidence to show in what year the visit which forms the subject of the representations was made; but as the twelfth year of Akhnaton's reign is mentioned in this tomb, it is probable that the visit took place somewhere about that time.

The queen must now have been between fifty and sixty years of age,[1] and her daughter Baketaton, born just before the death of her husband, was probably not much more than twelve years old. Akhnaton received his mother and sister with apparent joy and festivity, and the major-domo, Huya, was called upon to organise many a *fête* in their honour. Some of them are shown in the reliefs, where even the conventionalities of the artist have not been able to hide from us the luxury of the scene. One sees Akhnaton, his wife Nefertiti, his mother Tiy, his sister Baketaton, and his two daughters Merytaton and Ankhsenpaaton, seated together on comfortable cushioned chairs, their feet resting on elaborate footsools. Akhnaton is clad in a skirt of clinging linen, but the upper part of his body seems to have been bare.   On his forehead there gleams a small golden serpent, and on his feet there are elaborate sandals ; but

---

[1] It is probable, as has been stated on p. 111, that she was married to Amonhotep III. in about her tenth year, and was thus about forty-six when he died. She could not have been much more, for her daughter Baketaton must have been born but a year or so before Amonhotep's death, and it is improbable that she would bear children after forty-five, if as late as that.

with customary simplicity he wears no jewellery. Queen Nefertiti wears a flowing robe of fine linen, and on her forehead also there is the royal serpent. Queen Tiy wears the elaborate wig which was in vogue during the days of the old *régime*, and upon it there rests an ornamental crown consisting of a disk, two horns, two tall plumes, and two small serpents, probably all wrought in gold. A graceful robe of some almost transparent material falls lightly over her figure. The little girls appear to be naked.

Around this happy family group there stand graceful tables upon which food of all kinds is heaped. Here are joints of meat, dishes of confectionery, vegetables, fruit,[1] bread, cakes of various kinds, and so on. The tables are massed with lotus - flowers, according to the charming custom of the ancient Egyptians of all periods. Beside the tables stand jars of wine and other drinkables, festooned with ribbons. At the moment selected by the artist for reproduction, Akhnaton is seen placing his teeth in

---

[1] It is to be noticed that there are pomegranates amongst the fruit, which indicates that the visit was made during the summer, as do the light costumes also.

the neatly trimmed meat adhering to a large bone which he holds in his hand. To this day it is the custom in Egypt thus to eat with the hands. Nefertiti has a small roast duck in her hands at which she daintily nibbles. Tiy's morsel cannot now be seen, but as she places it to her mouth with one hand she presents a portion to her daughter, Baketaton, with the other. The two little princesses feed by Nefertiti's side, and appear to be sharing the meal. Meanwhile Huya hurries to and fro superintending the banquet, carefully tasting each dish before it is presented to the royal party. Two string bands play alternately, the one Egyptian and the other apparently Syrian. The former consists of four female performers, the first playing on a harp, the second and third on lutes, and the fourth on a lyre. The main instrument in the foreign band is a large standing lyre, about six feet in height, having eight strings, and being played with both hands. Courtiers clad in elaborate dresses, and holding ostrich-plume standards, are grouped around the hall in which the banquet takes place.

Another set of reliefs in the tomb of Huya shows us an evening entertainment in honour of Queen Tiy. Again the same members of the royal family are represented, but against the cool night air more clothes are worn by each person, and the upper part of the king's body is now seen to be covered by a mantle of soft linen. The king, queen, and queen-dowager are all shown drinking from delicate bowls, probably made of gold. This being an evening festival, little solid food appears to have been eaten, but there are three flower-decked tables piled high with fruit. From these the little princesses, now wearing light garments, help themselves liberally; and the small Ankhsenpaaton stands upon the footstool of her mother's chair, holding on to her skirts with one hand, while with the other she crams an apricot or some similar fruit into her mouth. Two string bands make music as before, and again the groups of courtiers stand about the hall; while Huya hastens to and fro directing the waiters, who, with napkins thrown over their arms, replenish the drinking-bowls from the wine-jars. The hall is lit by several flaming lamps set upon tall stands, near each of which these jars have been placed.

8. TIY VISITS HER TEMPLE.

One more scene from this state visit is shown. Here we observe Akhnaton leading his mother affectionately by the hand to a temple which had been built in her honour, as her private place of worship, and which was called the "Shade of the Sun." This temple appears to have been a building of great beauty and considerable size. One passed through two great swinging doors fixed between the usual two pylons, and so entered the main court, which stood open to the sunlight. A pillared gallery passed along either side of this court, and between each of the columns there stood statues of Akhnaton, Amonhotep III., and Queen Tiy. In the middle of the court rose the altar, to which one mounted by a flight of low steps. At the far end of the court another set of pylons and swinging doors led into the inner chambers. Passing through these doors one entered a small gallery, on either side of which there were again statues of the Pharaoh and his mother. Beyond stood the sanctuary, closed by swinging doors; and inside this was the second altar, flanked by statues of the king and queen-dowager. To right and left of the sanctuary there were small chapels; and a passage led round behind the sanctuary to the usual shrines, where more royal statues were to be seen.

The building seems to have been brilliant with colours; and on this particular occasion the altars were heaped up with offerings. Great jars of wine, decked with garlands of flowers and ribbons, stood in the shadow of the colonnades; and meat, bread, fruit, and vegetables were piled on delicate stands, ornamented with flowers.

Akhnaton and Tiy were accompanied by the little Princess Baketaton, Akhnaton's sister, and her two ladies-in-waiting. Before them walked the queen's major-domo, Huya, accompanied by a foreign official wearing what appears to be Cretan costume.[1] Behind them walked a noble group of courtiers bearing ostrich-plume fans

[1] Davies: Amarna, iii. 8, note 1.

and standards; and outside the temple precincts waited a crowd of policemen, servants, charioteers and grooms in charge of the royal chariots, fan-bearers, porters, and temple attendants. These people shout and cheer loyally as the royal party arrives. "The ruler of the Aton!" they cry. "He shall exist for ever and ever!" "She who rises in beauty!" "To him on whom the Aton rises!" "She who is patron of this temple of Aton!" The old queen must have felt as though she were back once more in the days of her glory; and yet how different the simplicity of the religious ceremonies to those of the old priests of Amon - Ra. There was now but a prayer or two at the altar, a little burning of incense, a little bowing of the head, and then the procession back to the palace, and the silent closing of the holy gates.

9. THE DEATH OF QUEEN TIY.

It is possible that Queen Tiy took up her residence at the City of the Horizon in recognition of the lavish arrangements which her son had made for her. But whether this is so or not, it does not seem that she lived very long to enjoy such renewals of the pomps which she had known in her younger days. Her death appears to have taken place shortly after these celebrations, and, probably by her express commands, she was embalmed at Thebes and carried from her palace up the winding valley to the royal burying-ground amongst the rugged Theban hills. Akhnaton showed his affection for her by presenting the furniture for the tomb, and in the inscriptions on the outer coffin one reads that "he made it for his mother." The queen-dowager had evidently expressed a wish to be buried near her father and mother, Yuaa and Tuau; for the tomb, which is situated on the east side of the valley, is within a stone's-throw of the sepulchre where they lay. It was entered by a steep flight of steps leading down to a sloping passage, at the end of which was the large burial chamber, the walls of which were carefully whitewashed. On passing into this chamber a great box-like shrine, or outer coffin, was to be found, occupying the greater part of the room. The door to the shrine was made of costly cedar of Lebanon covered with gold, and was fitted with an ornamental bolt. Many of the nails which held the woodwork together were made of pure gold,—a fact which plainly shows us the wealth of the royal treasuries at this time. Scenes were embossed on the panels showing the queen standing under the rays of the Aton. The shrine itself was also made of cedar, covered with gold, and on all sides were scenes of the Aton worship. Here Akhnaton was shown with Tiy, and the life-giving rays of the sun streamed around their naturally drawn figures. Inside this outer box the coffin containing the great queen's mummy was laid. The usual funeral furniture was placed at the sides of the room : gaily coloured boxes, alabaster vases, faience toilet-pots, statuettes, &c. Some of the toilet utensils were made in the form of little figures of the grotesque god Bes, which indicates that Akhnaton still tolerated the recognition by other persons of some of the old gods. In the inscriptions upon the outer coffin he had been careful to call his father, Amonhotep III., by his second name, Nebmaara, as often as possible, in order to avoid the writing of the word Amon, his dislike of everything to do with that god being profound. He allowed it to be written, however, here and there, as it seemed right to him that it should appear. Akhnaton's prejudice against the old state god is also shown in another manner. Amon's consort was the goddess Mut "the Mother," whose name is written in hieroglyphs by a sign representing a vulture. Now when the inscription mentioned the king's *mother*, Tiy, the word *mut*, "mother," had to be written; but in order to avoid a similarity — even in spelling — to the name of the goddess, Akhnaton had the word written out phonetically, letter by letter, and thus dispensed with the use of the vulture sign.[1] Again, in the name Nebmaara, the meaning of which is "Ra, Lord of Truth," the sign *maa*, "truth," represented the goddess of that name. Akhnaton's religion was much concerned with the quality of truth, which he regarded as one of the greatest necessities to happiness and well-being; and the fallacy of supposing that there was an actual deity of truth was particularly

[1] This is to be observed also in some other inscriptions of the period.

apparent to him. He was, therefore, careful to write the sign *maa* in letters instead of with the hieroglyph of the goddess.

When the funeral ceremonies came to an end, when the last prayer was said and the last cloud of incense had floated to the roof, the golden door of the shrine was shut and bolted, the outer doorways were walled up, and an avalanche of stones, let down from the chippings heaped near by, obliterated all traces of the entrance. Thus Akhnaton paid his last tribute to his mother and to the originator, it may be, of the schemes which he had carried into effect; and his last link with the past was severed. With the death of this good woman a restraining influence, as kindly as it was powerful, slipped from his arm, and a new and fiercer chapter of his short life began.

VI.

THE THIRTEENTH TO THE FIFTEENTH
YEARS OF THE REIGN OF AKHNATON.

"The episode of the retirement of the king with his whole court to the new palace and city, . . . and the strange life of religious and artistic propaganda which he led there, . . . is one of the most curious and interesting in the history of the world."—BUDGE : 'History of Egypt.'

1. THE DEVELOPMENT OF THE RELIGION
OF ATON.

IN the Pharaoh's hymn to the Aton we read these words—

"Thou didst create the earth according to Thy desire, . . .
    The countries of Syria and Nubia,
    The land of Egypt. . . ."

It is certainly worthy of note that Syria and Nubia are thus named before Egypt, and seem to take precedence in Akhnaton's mind. In the same hymn the following lines occur :—

"The Nile in heaven is for the strangers, . . .
    But the Nile [itself,] it cometh from the nether world for Egypt."

Here Akhnaton refers to the rain which falls in Syria to water the lands of the stranger, and compares it with the river which irrigates his own country. Thus again his thoughts are first for Syria and then for Egypt. This is the true imperial spirit : in the broadness of the Pharaoh's mind his foreign possessions claim as much attention as do his own dominions, and demand as much love. The sentiments are entirely opposed to those of the earlier kings of this dynasty, who ground down the land of the "miserable" foreigner and extracted therefrom all its riches, without regard to aught else.

Akhnaton believed that his God was the Father of all mankind, and that the Syrian and the Nubian were as much under His protection as the Egyptian. This is a greater advance in ethics than may be at once apparent; for the Aton thus becomes the first deity who was not tribal or not national ever conceived by mortal mind. This is the Christian's, understanding of God, though not the Hebrew conception of Jehovah. This is the spirit which sends the missionary to the uttermost parts of the earth ; and it was such an attitude of mind which now

led Akhnaton to build a temple for the Aton
in the heart of Syria, and another far up in
the Sudan.[1] The site of the Syrian temple is
now lost, but the Nubian buildings were recently
discovered and seem to have been of considerable extent.

At the same time temples were being erected
in various parts of Egypt. At Hermonthis a
temple named " Horizon of Aton in Hermonthis "
was built; at Heliopolis there was a temple
named "Exaltation of Ra in Heliopolis," and
also a palace for the king; at Hermopolis and
at Memphis temples were erected; and in the
Fayum and the Delta "Houses" of Aton sprang
up. Few real converts, however, seem to have
been made; for the religion was far above the
understanding of the people. In deference to
the king's wishes the Aton was accepted, but
no love was shown for the new form of worship;
and, indeed, not even in the City of the Horizon itself was it understood.

A certain change was now made by Akhnaton
in the name of the Aton. The words "Heat
which is in Aton" did not seem to him to be

[1] Breasted : History of Egypt, p. 364.

very happily chosen. They had been used in the earliest years of the movement, and had evidently not been coined by Akhnaton himself. The word "heat" was in spelling very reminiscent of the name of one of the old gods, and, to the uninitiate, might suggest some connection. The name of the Aton was therefore changed to "Effulgence which comes from Aton," the new words introducing into the spelling the hieroglyph of Ra, the sun. The exact significance of the alteration is not known; but one may suppose that the new words better conveyed the meaning which Akhnaton wished to imply. Even now it is not easy to find a phrase to express that vital energy, that first cause of life, which the king so clearly understood.

The date of this change is somewhat uncertain, though it is definitely to be placed between the tenth and thirteenth year of the reign, the probability being that it took place at the end of the twelfth year, when Akhnaton was about twenty-three years old. The inscriptions upon the outer coffin, or shrine, of Queen Tiy show the older form of wording, and the change, therefore, took place after her death. Now the queen did not die till the middle or end of the twelfth year, for in the tomb of Huya events of that year are recorded,[1] and he still holds the office of steward to the queen, while a letter from Dushratta, mentioning Tiy, was docketed in the twelfth year. On the other hand, the new name of the Aton occurs in tombs which, by the number of Akhnaton's daughters represented in them, might be thought to have been constructed earlier than this.[2] Thus there is a slight discrepancy; but the point of significance is that the change occurred after the queen's death, and was thus concurrent with another change which must here be recorded.

2. AKHNATON OBLITERATES THE NAME OF AMON.

Up till this time it will have been observed that Akhnaton had behaved with great leniency

---

[1] Page 177.

[2] It is usual to date the tombs roughly by the number of daughters shown, presuming that the artist represented all the children living at the time. But though this gives us the lowest possible year, it does not always give us the highest, for daughters are obviously sometimes omitted when the available space was cramped.

towards the worshippers of the older gods, and
had not even persecuted the priesthood of Amon-
Ra.   It now becomes apparent that this restraint
was due to his mother's influence, for no sooner
was she dead than Akhnaton turned with the
fierceness of a fanatic upon the latter institution.
He issued an order that the name of Amon was
to be erased wherever it occurred, and this order
was carried out with such amazing thorough-
ness that hardly a single occurrence of the
name was overlooked.   Although thousands of
inscriptions, accessible to Akhnaton's agents, are
now known in which the name of Amon
occurs, there are but a few examples in which
the god's name has not been mutilated.   His
agents hammered the name out on the walls
of the temples throughout Egypt; they penetrated into the tombs of the dead to erase it
from the texts; they searched through the
minute inscriptions upon small statuettes and
figures, obliterating the name therefrom; they
made journeys into the distant deserts to cut
out the name from the rock-scribbles of travel-
lers; they clambered over the cliffs beside the
Nile to erase it from the graffiti; they entered

private houses to rub it from small utensils
where it chanced to be inscribed.

Akhnaton was always thorough in his under-
takings, and half-measures were unknown to
him. When it came to the question of his own
father's name, he seems not to have hesitated
to order the obliteration of the word Amon in
it, though one may suppose that in most cases
he painted over it the king's second name,
Nebmaara. His agents burst their way into
the tomb of Queen Tiy and removed the name
Amonhotep from the inscriptions upon the shrine,
writing Nebmaara in red ink over each erasure.
Having scratched out the name even upon one
of the queen's toilet-pots of minute size they
retired from the tomb, building up the wall at
the entrance, and continued their labours elsewhere. The king was now asked whether his
own name, Amonhotep, — which had been used
before he adopted the better known Akhnaton,
—was to suffer the same fate, and the answer
seems to have been in the affirmative. Upon
the quarry tablet at Gebel Silsileh [1] the king's
discarded name is thus erased, though it was

[1] Page 63.

not damaged in the tomb of Rames. The names
of the various nobles and officials, male and
female, which were compounded with Amon—
Amonhotep, Setamon, Amonemhat, Amonemapt,
and so on — were ruthlessly destroyed; while
living persons bearing such names were often
obliged to change them.

In thus mutilating his father's name Akhnaton
did not in any way intend to disparage his
forbears. He was but desirous of utterly obliterating Amon from the memory of man, in
order that the true God might the better receive acceptance. He was proud of his descent,
and, unlike most of his ancestors, he showed a
desire to honour the memory of his father. We
have seen[1] how one of his artists, Bek, represented the figure of Amonhotep III. upon
his monument at Aswan. Huya, Queen Tiy's
steward, was authorised by Akhnaton to show
that king upon the walls of his tomb;[2] and in
the private temple of Queen Tiy, it will be remembered that there were statues of Amonhotep III.[3] Likewise, the earlier kings of the

---

[1] Page 107.   [2] Davies : El Amarna, iii., Pl. xviii.
[3] Page 182.

dynasty received unusual recognition.   An official
named Any held the office of Steward of the
House of Amonhotep II.;[1] and there is a representation of Akhnaton offering to Aton in "the
House of Thothmes IV. in the City of the Horizon."[2]   Upon his boundary tablet Akhnaton
refers to Amonhotep III. and Thothmes IV. as
being troubled by the priesthood of Amon.

It would seem from the above that there were
shrines dedicated to Akhnaton's ancestors in the
City of the Horizon, each of which had its
steward and its officials; and it is probable
that Akhnaton arranged that a memorial shrine
of the same kind should be erected for himself
against his death, for we read of a personage
who was "Second Priest" of the king.[3]   It was
his desire in this manner to show the continuity
of his descent from the Pharaohs of the elder
days, and to demonstrate his real claim to that
title "Son of the Sun" which had been held
by the sovereigns of Egypt ever since the Fifth
Dynasty, and which was of such vital import-

[1] Davies : El Amarna.
[2] Wilkinson : Modern Egypt, ii. 69.
[3] Davies : El Amarna.

ance in the new religion. It was in this manner that he claimed descent from Ra, who was to him the same with Aton; and just as the great religious teachers of the Hebrews made careful note of their genealogies in order to prove themselves descended from Adam, and hence in a manner from God, so Akhnaton thus demonstrated the continuity of his line in order to show his real right to the titles "Child of Aton" and "Son of the Sun."

3. THE GREAT TEMPLE OF ATON.

The City of the Horizon of Aton must now have been a very city of temples. There were these shrines dedicated to the king's ancestors; there was the temple of Queen Tiy; there was a shrine for the use of Baketaton, the king's sister; there was the "House of putting the Aton to Rest," where Queen Nefertiti officiated; and there was the great temple of Aton, in which probably were included other of the buildings named in the inscriptions. The great temple may here be briefly described, as the reader has so far made the acquaintance only of the building belonging to Queen Tiy.

The temple was entirely surrounded by a high wall, and in this respect was not unlike the existing temple of Edfu, which the visitor to Egypt will assuredly have seen. Inside the area thus enclosed there were two buildings, the one behind the other, standing clear of the walls, thus leaving a wide ambulatory around them. Upon passing through the gates of the enclosing wall there was seen before one the façade of the first of the two temples, while to right and left there stood a small lodge or vestry. The façade of the temple was most imposing. Two great pylons towered up before one, rising from behind a pillared portico, and between them stood the gateway with its swinging doors. Up the face of each pylon shot five tall masts, piercing the blue sky above, and from the heads of each there fluttered a crimson pennant. Passing through the gateway one entered an open court, in the midst of which stood the high altar, up to which a flight of steps ascended. On either side of this sun-bathed enclosure stood a series of small chapels or chambers; while in front of one, in the axial line, there was another gateway leading on into the second court, from which one passed again into a third court. ‎ Passing through yet another gateway, a fourth division of the temple was reached, this being a pillared gallery or colonnade where one might rest for a while in the cool shadow. Then onwards through another gateway into the fifth court, crossing which one entered the sixth court, where stood another altar in the full sunshine. A series of some twenty little chambers passed around the sides of this court, and looking into the darkness beyond each of their doorways one might discern the simple tables and stands with which the rooms were furnished. A final gateway now led one into the seventh and last court, where again there was an altar, and again a series of chambers surrounded the open space.

Behind this main temple, and quite separate from it though standing within the one enclosure, stood the lesser temple, which was probably the more sacred of the two. It was fronted by a pillared portico, and before each column stood a statue of Akhnaton, beside which was a smaller figure of his wife or one of his daughters. Passing through the gateway, which was so designed that nothing beyond could be seen, one entered an open court in which stood the altar, and around the sides of which were small chambers. Here the temple ended, save for a few chambers of uncertain use, approached from the ambulatory.

Both buildings were gay with colours, and at festivals there were numerous stands heaped high with flowers and other offerings, while red ribbons added their notes of brilliant colour on all sides. There was nothing gloomy or sombre in this temple of Aton; and it contrasts strikingly with the buildings in which Amon was worshipped. There vast halls were lit by minute windows, and a dim uncertainty hovered around the worshipper. Such temples lent themselves to mystery, and amidst their gloomy shadows many a supplicant's heart beat in terror. Dark stairways led to subterranean passages, and these passages to black chambers built in the thickness of the wall, from whence the hollow voice of the priest throbbed as from mid-air upon the ears of the crouching congregation. But in Akhnaton's temple each court was open to the full blaze of the sun-

light.[1] There was, there could be, no mystery ;
nor could there be any terror of darkness to
loosen the knees of the worshipper. Akhnaton,
true scientist that he was, had no sympathy for
the occult and no interest in spiritualism. Boldly
he looked to God as a child to its father ; and
having solved what he deemed to be the riddle
of life, there was no place in his mind for aught
but an open, fearless adoration of the Creator
of that vital energy which he saw in all things.
Akhnaton was the sworn enemy of the table-
turners of his day, and the tricks of priestcraft,
the stage effects of religiosity, were anathema
to his pure mind.

4. THE BEAUTY OF THE CITY.

The City of the Horizon of Aton was now a
place of surpassing beauty. Eight or nine years
of lavish expenditure in money and skill had
transformed the fields and the wilderness into

---

[1] It is probable that there was some likeness between Akhnaton's
temples and those dedicated to the sun in early days, as, for example
that at Abusêr.

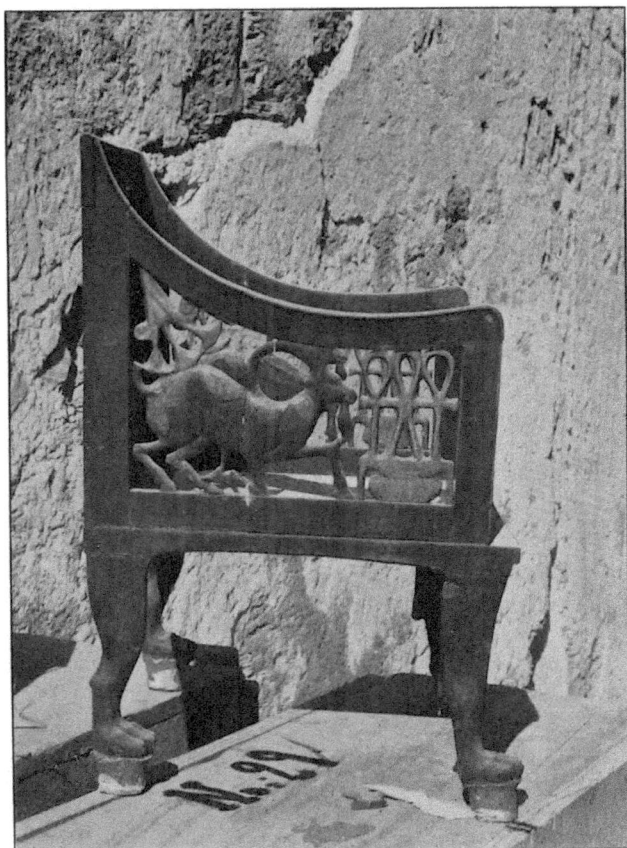

Carved Wooden Chair, the designs partly covered with gold-leaf.

as fair a city as the world had ever seen. One of the nobles who lived there, by name May, describes it in these words: "The mighty City of the Horizon of Aton, great in loveliness, mistress of pleasant ceremonies, rich in possessions, the offering of the sun being in her midst. At the sight of her beauty there is rejoicing. She is lovely and beautiful: when one sees her it is like a glimpse of heaven."

There was almost constant music in her streets, and the scent of flowers was wafted upon every breeze. Besides the temples and public buildings the city was adorned with numerous palaces, each standing in fair gardens. One of these mansions,[1] represented in the tomb of Meryra, seems to have constituted a happy combination of comfort and simplicity, as may be seen from its pictures. One entered a walled court, and so passed to the main entrance of the house. A portico, the roof of which was supported by four decorative columns festooned with ribbons, sheltered the elaborate doorway from the sunshine. Passing through this doorway, from the top of which a row of cobras gleamed down

[1] Perhaps this is a part of the royal palace.

upon one, a pillared hall was reached; and beyond this the visitor entered the great dining- .
hall.   Twelve columns supported the ceiling,
which was probably painted with flights of
birds; and under a kind of kiosk in the middle
of the hall stood the dining-table and several comfortable arm-chairs, cushioned in bright colours.
Beyond this hall there was a court, at the back
of which were several chambers, one being a
bedroom, as a great cushioned bedstead clearly
shows.   The owner's womenfolk probably occupied another portion of the building not shown
in the representations.

The palace of Ay, Akhnaton's father-in-law,
was a more pretentious building.   It was entered
by a fine doorway which led into a. court.   A
second door gave entrance to the large, pillared
dining-hall, and through this one passed into a
court from which bedrooms and boudoirs led off.
In one of these rooms two women, clad in airy
garments, are seen to be dancing with one
another, while a man plays a harp.   In another
room a girl likewise dances to the strains of a
harp, while a servant dresses the hair of one of
the gentlemen of the household.   Other rooms

contain lutes, harps, and lyres, as well as objects of the toilet. A little court is now reached, where fragrant flowers grow, and tanks of water, sunk in the decorated pavement, give a sense of coolness to the air. Beyond this are more apartments, and finally the kitchens are reached. Throughout the house stand delicate tables upon which jars of wine or dishes of fruit are to be seen; and cushioned arm-chairs, with footstools before them, are ready for the weary. Servants are seen passing to and fro bearing refreshments, or stopping to dust the floor, or again idly talking in the passages.

Akhnaton's palace is not very clearly shown in the tomb reliefs or paintings, but portions of it were found in the modern excavations on the site.[1] Like all the residential buildings of the period, it was an airy and light structure made of brick. The walls, ceilings, and floors were covered with the most beautiful paintings; and delicate pillars, inlaid with coloured glass and stone, or covered with realistically painted vines and creepers, supported the light rooves of its halls. Portions of the pavement are still

[1] Petrie: El Amarna.

preserved, and the visitor to the site of the city may still see the paintings there depicted. A young calf, frisking in the sunlight, gallops through a field of red poppies; wild geese rise from the marshes and beat their way through the reeds, disturbing the butterflies as they do so; amidst the lotus-flowers resting upon the rippling water the sinuous fish are seen to wander. These are but fragments of the paintings which once delighted the eyes of the Pharaoh, or brought a sigh to the lips of his queen.

The art of the painter of this period excels in the depiction of animal and plant life. The winding, tangled stems and leaves of vines were carefully studied; the rapid motions of animals were correctly caught; and it has been said that in these things the artists of Akhnaton were greater than those in any other Oriental art.[1] Sculpture in the round, too, reached a pitch of excellence never before known. The statue of Akhnaton illustrated opposite is the work of one who may rank with Donatello, if not with Cellini.

[1] Petrie: History of Egypt, ii. 219.

Akhnaton.
(From a statuette in the Louvre.)

Death Mask of Akhnaton.

It is possible that Auta, the chief sculptor of Queen Tiy,[1] is the creator of this statue, and perhaps also of the head, probably, of Akhnaton's daughter shown opposite next page. In the tomb of Huya there is a scene representing this artist seated in his studio giving the final touches to a statue of Princess Baketaton. He sits upon a low stool, palette in hand, and, as was the custom, colours the surface of the statue. Unlike the stiff conventional poses of earlier work, the attitude of the young girl is easy and graceful. One hand hangs by her side : in the other she holds a pomegranate, which she is about to raise to her lips. Auta's assistant stands beside the figure, and near by two apprentices work upon objects of less importance, their chisels on a table by their side.

Works such as these which Auta and his companions were turning out are permanent memorials of the reign of Akhnaton, which will carry his name through the years until, as he would say, "the swan turns black and the crow turns white." There must surely come a time, and soon, when the art of Egypt will receive

[1] Page 75.

more attention; and one may then hear Akhnaton's name coupled with that of the Medici as
the patron, if not the teacher, of great masters.
It was he who released them from convention,
and bade their hands repeat what their eyes
saw; and it was he who directed those eyes to
the beauties of nature around them. He, and
no other, taught them to look at the world in
the spirit of life, to infuse into the cold stone
something of the "effulgence which comes from
Aton"; and, if these few treasures which have
survived the utter wreck of the City of the
Horizon have put one's heart to a happy step,
it was Akhnaton who first set the measure.

5. AKHNATON'S AFFECTION FOR HIS FAMILY.

In about the thirteenth year of the reign a fifth
daughter was born, who was named Neferneferura.
This seems to have been the first daughter born
after the changes in the religion recorded at
the beginning of this chapter[1] had taken place;
and it is significant that the name of Aton, of
which all the previous daughters' names had

---

[1] Page 192.

Head of Akhnaton's Daughter.

been compounded, now gives place to Ra. A sixth daughter seems to have made her appearance somewhat over a year later, some time during the fourteenth year of the reign. Again Ra is used in the name instead of Aton, she being called Setepenra. It is impossible to say what was the meaning of this slight change in the theological aspect of the religion at this period, but it seems evident that certain developments in which Ra figured were now introduced.

No son was yet forthcoming, and both the king and the queen must now have suffered six successive disappointments. It may be mentioned here that the next child born to the unfortunate couple in the following year proved to be a seventh girl and a seventh disappointment; and in the remaining two years of the reign no other child was born, or at any rate was weaned, so that Akhnaton died sonless. It is strange to picture this lofty-minded preacher in his home, with his six little girls around him, as he is shown upon the monuments. No other Pharaoh thus portrayed himself surrounded by his family; but Akhnaton seems to have never been happy unless all his children were with him and his wife by his side. The charm of family life, and the sanctity of the relationship of husband and wife, parents and children, seems to have been an important point of doctrine to him. He urged his nobles, also, to give their attention to their families; and in the tomb of Panehesy, for example, one may see representations of that personage sitting with his wife and his three daughters around him.

Akhnaton's affection for his daughters is now shown to us in another manner. When Amon-hotep III. had asked the King of Mitanni for one of his daughters to be given in marriage to Akhnaton, the little Nefertiti was at once dispatched, although she was not yet old enough to cohabit with her husband. He had no scruples about sending the child of eight years old to a foreign country, and seems to have packed her off without a thought. Now, however, we obtain a glimpse of Akhnaton's actions under similar circumstances, and the difference is marked. The King of Babylon, Burraburiash, wrote to Akhnaton in about the fourteenth or fifteenth year of the reign, asking for one of the Pharaoh's daughters as a wife for his son. Wishing to be on friendly terms with Babylonia, Akhnaton consented to the union, and selected probably his fourth daughter, Nefer-nefernaton, as the future Queen of Babylon. His eldest daughter subsequently married a noble named Smenkhkara, who succeeded to the throne after the death of Akhnaton; and his third daughter was later married to another noble named Tutankhaton, who usurped the throne, as we shall see in the sequel. The fact that neither of these daughters was now chosen to marry the Babylonian prince indicates that they were already betrothed to their future husbands, and hence this event could not have taken place much earlier than at the date mentioned above. The second daughter, Meke-taton, was not selected for the reason that she seems to have been in a precarious state of health. The little princess who was chosen was born in the tenth year of the reign, and was now not more than five years of age. Akhnaton, unlike the King of Mitanni, did not at once send the child to her future home, but arranged the marriage by proxy, and thus kept his daughter with him for yet a few years. This is made evident from the fact that in a letter from Burraburiash to Akhnaton, the Babylonian king states that he is sending a necklace of over a thousand stones to the "Pharaoh's daughter, the wife of his son," who is thus evidently still resident in Egypt.

Besides Akhnaton's six, and presently seven, daughters there were two other princesses probably in residence at the palace. One of these, his young sister Baketaton, whom we have seen visiting the City of the Horizon with her mother, is not again heard of, and perhaps did not long survive the dowager-queen's death. The other was Nezemmut, the sister of Queen Nefertiti, who seems to have lived in Egypt continuously since the time of the founding of the new city, when we last saw her.[1] Her portraits are shown in the tombs of May, Panebesy, and Ay; and she is generally seen to be accompanied by two female dwarfs, named Para and Reneheh, who appear to have waddled

[1] She probably married some Egyptian noble, and her future career is recorded on p. 269.

after her wherever she went. She was still, no
doubt, very young, and these two grotesque
attendants were entrusted with her safety as
well as her amusement.

6. AKHNATON'S FRIENDS.

The simple and homely manner in which
Akhnaton is represented by his artists, surrounded by his children, is an indication that
although he demanded much homage from his
subjects in his capacity as their Pharaoh, he but
asked for their sympathy and affection in all
other connections. As Pharaoh his person was
inapproachable and his attitude aloof, but as a
man he never failed to set an example of what
he considered a man should do; and even upon
his throne, to which one might but advance
with bowed head and bended knee, he displayed
his mortal nature to all beholders by joking with
his children or paying fond attention to his
wife. So, also, many of his disciples and courtiers, who so ceremoniously approached the steps
of his throne, were in reality his good friends

and intimates. Akhnaton did not care a snap of the fingers for aristocratic traditions, and although he demanded the conventional respect of his subjects, and upheld the less tiresome rules of court etiquette, many of his closest friends were of peasant origin, and the hands which now held the jewelled ostrich-plume standards could as easily grasp the pick or the plough.

May, a high official of the city, speaks of himself in the following words: "I was a man of low origin both on my father's and on my mother's side, but the King established me. . . . He caused me to grow . . . by his bounty when I was a man of no property; . . . he gave me food and provisions every day, I who had been one that begged bread." Huya, Queen Tiy's steward, speaks of the king as selecting his officials from the ranks of the yeomen. Panehesy tells us that Akhnaton is one "who maketh princes and formeth the humble," and he adds: "When I knew not the companionship of princes I was made an intimate of the King." But if the Pharaoh raised men from the ranks, he was also capable of degrading those who offended against the standards which he had set up.   Thus May seems to have been disgraced and turned out of the city.

The tomb of the police official, Mahu, who was a favourite of the king, though probably not of exalted origin, has provided us with some scenes relating to his official work which are of considerable interest.   In one series of these we are shown the capture of some foreigners, or perhaps Beduin, who may have belonged to some gang of thieves or anarchists.   Mahu has been awakened in the early hours of a winter morning by the news of the disturbance, and as he listens to the report a servant blows a small fire into flame, since the morning air is chilly.   He then sends for his chariot and drives to the scene of the crime, whatever it may be; and soon he has effected the arrest of some of the culprits. These men are then conveyed to the Vizir, who, with his staff, receives Mahu with exclamations of approval.   "Examine these men, O Princes," says the police officer, "whom the foreigners have instigated."   From these words it might seem that the prisoners were foreign spies, or even assassins plotting against the life of the Pharaoh.

Whether from fear of a revolt in Egypt or from mere custom, the City of the Horizon was closely defended at this time, and there is a scene in this same tomb in which Akhnaton is shown inspecting the fortifications. He drives in his chariot with his wife and his eldest daughter Merytaton; and although the spirited horses would appear to be difficult to manage, the more so because the mischievous Merytaton is poking them with a stick, Akhnaton is a sufficiently good driver to be able to carry on a conversation with the queen, and to address a few words to Mahu, who runs by the side of the chariot. In striking contrast to the custom of other Pharaohs, Akhnaton is accompanied by an unarmed bodyguard of police as he drives round the defences; and in this we may perhaps see an indication of his popularity. The fortifications, it may be noted, consist of blockhouses built at regular intervals, and defended by wire or rope entanglements.

In several of the tombs there are representations of their owners receiving rewards from the king for their diligence in their official works, or for their intelligent acceptance of his teaching. A high official named Pentu has left us a scene in which Akhnaton is shown seated in the hall of his palace, while Pentu stands before him to receive numerous golden collars at the royal hands in recognition of his services. A part of the palace is shown, but the scene is much damaged: a small pond or tank surrounded by flowers is shown in one corner of the enclosure, but the plan of the various rooms is confused, and is quite subsidiary to the representation of the hall where the Pharaoh receives the happy Pentu. Akhnaton seems to have been a good friend, as he was a stern enemy; and those who assisted him in the difficult tasks which he had set himself were lavishly rewarded for their pains.

7. AKHNATON'S TROUBLES.

Akhnaton's health was so very uncertain that he hastened to construct for himself a tomb in the cliffs behind the City of the Horizon. He selected as the site of his last resting-place a gaunt and rugged valley which here cuts

into the hills, leading back, around tumbled
rocks and up dry watercourses, to the Arabian
desert beyond.   It is

> "A savage place !—as holy and enchanted
> As e'er beneath a waning moon was haunted
> By woman wailing for her demon-lover."

Here Akhnaton elected to be buried, where
hyænas prowled and jackals wandered, and where
the desolate cry of the night - owls echoed over
the rocks.   In winter the cold wind sweeps
up this valley and howls around the rocks ;
in summer the sun makes of it a veritable
furnace unendurable to man.   There is nothing
here to remind one of the God who watches
over him, and the tender Aton of the Pharaoh's
conception would seem to have abandoned this
place to the spirits of evil.   There are no flowers
where Akhnaton cut his sepulchre, and no birds
sing ; for the king believed that his soul, caught
up into the noon of Paradise, would need no
more the delights of earth.

The tomb consisted of a passage descending
into the hill, and leading to a rock - cut hall,
the roof of which was supported by four columns.
Here stood the sarcophagus of pink granite in

which the Pharaoh's mummy would lie. The walls of this hall were covered with scenes carved in plaster,[1] representing various phases of the Aton worship. From the passage there led another small chamber beyond which a further passage was cut, perhaps to lead to a second hall in which the queen should be buried; but the work was never finished.

The construction of the tomb was interrupted by the death of Akhnaton's second daughter, Meketaton, who had barely lived to see her ninth birthday. It has already been seen that she seems to have been ailing for some time, and her death was perhaps no surprise to her parents. Their grief, however, was none the less acute for this; and when the body of the little girl had been laid to rest in one of the chambers of her father's tomb, the walls were covered at Akhnaton's order with scenes representing the grief of the bereaved family. Here Queen Nefertiti is seen holding in her

---

[1] The plaster has now fallen off, and little of the original decoration remains. The tomb is seldom visited by tourists, being seven miles back from the river; but it is in charge of the Government custodian.

arms her lately born seventh daughter, whose name, ending in . . . t, is now lost; while the five other little girls weep with their parents beside the bier of their dead sister. It is a pathetic picture, and one which stirs our sympathy for a Pharaoh who, unlike all other kings of Egypt, could weep for the loss of a daughter.

This was not Akhnaton's only grief. His doctrines were not being accepted in Egypt as readily as he had hoped, and he was probably able to detect a considerable amount of insincerity in the attitude of those around him. There was hardly a man whom he could trust to continue in the faith should he himself die; and even as he put the last touches to his temples and his palaces he was aware that he had built his house upon the sand. The empire which he had dreamed of, bound together by the ties of a common worship of Aton, was fast fading out of sight, and the news which reached him from Syria was disquieting in the extreme.

At this time the King of Babylon, whose son had married Akhnaton's daughter, seems to have been on bad terms with his neighbour, the King of Mitanni, the father of the Pharaoh's much-loved Queen Nefertiti; and Akhnaton came nigh to being drawn into the quarrel. The Babylonian king had been ill for some time, and in the course of the international correspondence Nefertiti had never once sent her condolences to him, apparently because he was a poor friend to her father. This was much resented, and the King of Babylon at last sent an insulting letter to Akhnaton, in which he states that he is sending him the usual present of decorative objects which etiquette required of him, but that he wishes it to be understood that only a fraction of the gift is intended for the "mistress of his house," *i.e.*, Nefertiti, since she had not troubled to ask after his health.

Shortly after this he wrote another letter to Akhnaton making various complaints, and stating that his messengers had been robbed in territory belonging to the Pharaoh, who must therefore make good their losses. A third letter makes similar complaints, and hints at future trouble. Meanwhile the King of Mitanni was on none too friendly terms with Akhnaton, and appears to have detained the Pharaoh's envoy, named Mani, thereby causing Akhnaton considerable anxiety. There was, in fact, a general tendency to disparage the Egyptian king, which must have been exceedingly galling to Akhnaton, who had the power to let loose upon Asia an army which would silence all insult, but did not find such a step consistent with his principles. In a letter which he wrote to one of the Syrian princes whose fidelity was doubtful, Akhnaton ends his despatch with the words: "I am very well, I the sun in the heavens, and my chariots and soldiers are exceedingly numerous; and from Upper Egypt even unto Lower Egypt, and from the place where the sun riseth even unto the place where he setteth, the whole country is in good cause and content." Thus we see that Akhnaton knew his power, and wished that others should know it; and it is therefore the more surprising that, as we shall presently find, he never chose to use it.

VII.

THE LAST TWO YEARS OF THE REIGN OF AKHNATON.

"I know, he said, what you like is to look at the mountains, or to go up among them and kill things. But I like the running water in a quiet garden, with a rose reflected in it, and the nightingale singing to it. Listen!"—MIRZA MAHOMED in 'The Story of Valeh and Hadijeh.'

1. THE HITTITE INVASION OF SYRIA.

THE eastern end of the Mediterranean is bounded on the south by Egypt and the desert, on the east by Palestine and Syria, and on the north by Asia Minor, these roughly forming the three sides of a square. The conquests of the great warrior-Pharaoh Thothmes III. had carried the Egyptian power as far as the north-east corner of this formation—that is to say, to the point where Syria meets Asia Minor. The island of Cyprus is in shape not unlike a hand with index finger extended; and this finger may be said to be pointing to the limit of Egyptian conquest, somewhere in the neighbourhood of the Amanus Mountains. The kingdom of Mitanni, the home of Queen Nefertiti, was situated on the banks of the Euphrates some distance inland from these mountains; and as it acted as a buffer state between the Egyptian possessions in Syria and the unconquered lands beyond, the Pharaohs had taken care to unite themselves by marriage, as we have seen, with its rulers. Behind Mitanni to the north-east, the friendly kingdoms later known as Assyria marked the limits of the known world; while to the north the hostile lands of Asia Minor lay in the possession of the Hittites, a warlike confederacy of peoples, perhaps the ancestors of the modern Armenians. From these hardy warriors the greatest danger to the Egyptian Empire in Syria was to be expected; and the statesmen of Egypt must have cast many an anxious look towards those forbidding mountains which loomed beyond Mitanni. A southern movement of the Hittites, indications of which were already very apparent, would bring them swarming over and around the Amanus Mountains, either along the eastern and inland route through Mitanni, or along the western route beside the sea and over the Lebanon, or again, midway between these two routes, past the great cities of Tunip, Kadesh, and others, which stood to block the way.

When Akhnaton ascended the throne, Seplel was king of the Hittites, and was by way of being friendly to Egypt. Some of his people, however, crossed the frontiers of Mitanni and were repulsed by Dushratta, the king of that country, who was father-in-law to Akhnaton. This caused some coldness between Seplel and the Pharaoh; and although the former sent an embassy to the City of the Horizon, the correspondence between the two monarchs presently ceased. The young idealist of Egypt seems to have held warfare in horror; and the Hittites were so essentially a fighting race that Akhnaton could have had no friendly feelings towards them. Soon we find that these Hittites, unable to overflow into the land of Mitanni, have moved along the eastern route and have seized the land of Amki, which lay on the sea-coast between the Amanus Mountains and the Lebanon. This movement might have been stopped by Aziru,

an Amorite prince who ruled the territory between Amki and Mitanni, and whose duty, as
an Egyptian vassal, was to check the southern
incursions of the Hittites.   But Aziru, like his
father Abdashirta before him, was a man as
ambitious as he was faithless, and his dealings
both with the Hittites and with the Egyptians
during the following years were unscrupulous
in the extreme.   It was his policy to play the
one nation against the other, and to extend
the scope of his own power at the expense of
both.

2. AKHNATON'S CONSCIENTIOUS OBJECTIONS
TO WARFARE.

Akhnaton's policy in Syria, when considered
from the point of view of an ordinary man, was
of the weakest.   Ideals cannot govern an empire,
and those who would apply the doctrine of
" peace and goodwill" to subject races endanger
the very principles which they would teach.
While the young Pharaoh was singing his
imperial psalms to the Aton in his growing

capital, the princes of Syria were whistling the revolutionary ditties which presently were to ring in the ears of the isolated Egyptian garrisons. Little did they care for that tender Father of Mankind to whom Akhnaton's thin finger so earnestly pointed. They knew nothing of monotheism; they found no satisfaction in One who was the gentle ruler of all men without distinction of race. A true god to them was a vanquisher of other gods, a valiant leader in battle, a relentless avenger of insult. The furious Baal, the bloodthirsty Tishub, the terrible Ishtar — these were the deities that a man could love. How they scorned that God of Peace who was called the Only One! How they laughed at the young Pharaoh who had set aside the sword for the psalter, who hoped to rule his restless dominions by love alone!

Love! One stands amazed at the reckless idealism, the beautiful folly, of this Pharaoh who, in an age of turbulence, preached a religion of peace to seething Syria. Three thousand years later mankind is still blindly striving after these same ideals in vain. Now-

adays one is familiar with the doctrine : a
greater than Akhnaton has preached it, and
has died for it. To-day God is known to us,
and the peace of God is a thing hoped for ;
but at that far-off period, thirteen hundred
years before the birth of Christ, two or three
centuries before the age of David and Solomon,
and many a year before the preaching of Moses,
one is utterly surprised to behold the true light
shining forth for a short moment like the sun
through a rift in the clouds, and one knows
that it has come too soon.   Mankind, even now
not ready, was then most wholly unprepared,
and the price which Egypt paid for the ideals
of her Pharaoh was no less than the complete
loss of her dominions.

Akhnaton believed in God, and to him that
belief meant a practical abhorrence of war.
Marshalling the material available for the study
of this period of history, one can interpret the
events in Syria in only one way : Akhnaton
definitely refused to do battle, believing that
a resort to arms was an offence to God.
Whether fortune or misfortune, gain or loss,
was to be his lot, he would hold to his

principles, and would not return to the old gods of battle.

It must be remembered that at this time the empire was the personal property of the Pharaoh, as every kingdom was of its king. Nobody ever considered a possession as belonging to the nation which had laid hands upon it, but only to that nation's king. It mattered very little to the Syrian peoples whether their owner was an Egyptian or a Syrian, though perhaps they preferred to be possessed by one of their own race. Akhnaton was thus doing his will with his own property. He was refusing to fight for his own possessions; he was acting literally upon the Christian principle of giving the cloak to him who had stolen the coat. Patriotism was a sentiment unknown to the world: devotion to the king's personal interest was all that actuated loyalty in the subject, and the monarch himself had but his own interests to consider. Thus Akhnaton cannot be accused of ruining his country by his refusal to go to war. He was entitled to do what he liked with his own personal property, and if he sacrificed his possessions to his

principles, the sacrifice was made upon God's
high altar, and the loss would be felt by him
alone. Such a loss, it is true, would probably
break his heart; for he loved Syria dearly, and
he had had such great hopes of uniting the
empire by the tie of a common religion. But
for good or ill, · he was determined to stand
aloof from the struggles upon which Syria was
now entering.

3. THE FAITHLESSNESS OF AZIRU.

While Aziru, the Amorite, schemed on the
borders of Asia Minor, a Syrian prince named
Itakama suddenly set up an independent kingdom at Kadesh and joined hands with the
Hittites, thus cutting off the loyal city of Tunip,
the friendly kingdom of Mitanni, and the territory of the faithless Aziru from direct intercourse with the Lebanon and Egypt's remaining
possessions in Palestine and Syria. Three loyal
vassal kings, perhaps assisted by Dushratta of
Mitanni, attacked the rebels, but were repulsed
by Itakama and his Hittite allies.

Aziru at once turned the situation to his own advantage. Hemmed in between the Hittites on the north and this new kingdom of Kadesh on the south, he collected his armies and marched down the Orontes to the Mediterranean coast, capturing the cities near the mouth of that river and adding them. to his possessions. Should the Hittites ask him to give an account of these proceedings, he could reply that he was, as it were, the advance - guard of the Hittite invasion of Syria, and was preparing the road for them. Should Itakama question him, he could say- that he was, with friendly hands, linking the Hittites with Kadesh. And should Akhnaton call upon him for an explanation, he could answer that he was securing the land for the Egyptians against the Hittite advance.

No doubt Aziru preferred to keep his peace with the Hittites the most secure, for it was obvious that they were the rising people; but at the same time he did not yet dare to show any hostility to Egypt, whose armies might at any moment be launched across the Mediterranean. Unable to hold a position of independence, he now thought it most prudent to allow the northmen to swarm southwards through his dominions, from Amki over and around the Lebanon to Kadesh, where their ally Itakama dwelt. In return for this assistance he seems to have been allowed a free hand in the forwarding of his own interests, and we now find him turning his attention to the sea-coast cities of Simyra and Byblos, which nestled at the western foot of the Lebanon. Here, however, he received a check, and failed to obtain a footing. He therefore marched eastwards to the city of Niy, which he captured, slaying its king; and both to the Hittites and to the Egyptians he seems to have pretended that he had taken this step in their interests.

On hearing of the fall of this city the governor of Tunip wrote a pathetic appeal to Akhnaton, asking for help; for he was now quite isolated, and he knew that Aziru was a free-lance who cared not a jot for any but his own welfare.

"To the King of Egypt, my lord," runs the letter. "The inhabitants of Tunip, thy servant. May it be well with thee, and at the feet of our lord we fall. My lord, Tunip, thy servant, speaks, saying: Who formerly could have plundered Tunip without being plundered by Thothmes III.? The gods . . . of the King of Egypt, my lord, dwell in Tunip. May our lord ask his old men [if it be not so.] Now, however, we belong no more to our lord, the King of Egypt. . . . If his soldiers and chariots come too late, Aziru will make us like the city of Niy. If, however, we have to mourn, then the King of Egypt will mourn over these things which Aziru has done, for he will turn his hand against our lord. And when Aziru enters Simyra Aziru will do to us as he pleases, in the territory of our lord the King, and on account of these things our lord will have to lament. And now Tunip, thy city, weeps, and her tears are flowing, and there is no help for us. For twenty years we have been sending to our lord the King, the King of Egypt, but there has not come to us a word—no, not one."

Several points become apparent from this letter. One sees that in the more distant cities of Syria the significance of Akhnaton's new religion was not understood. The governor of Tunip refers to the old gods of Egypt worshipped in that town, and he knows not, or cannot be brought to believe, that Akhnaton has become a mono-theist. One sees that the memory of the terrible Thothmes III. and his victorious armies was still

in men's minds, and was probably one of the
main causes of the long-continued peace in Syria.
Akhnaton's father, Amonhotep III., had not concerned himself greatly with regard to his foreign
dominions, and, as the people of Tunip had been
asking for assistance for twenty years, it would
seem that the danger which now beset them
was already feared before that Pharaoh's death.

How, one asks, could Akhnaton read such a
letter as this, and yet refuse to send a relieving
army to Syria? Byblos and Simyra were still
loyally holding out; and troops disembarked at
these ports could speedily be marched inland to
Tunip, could crush Hakama at Kadesh, and
could frighten Aziru into giving real assistance
to Dushratta and other loyal kings in holding
the Hittites back behind the Amanus Mountains. But this was Akhnaton's Gethsemane, if
one may say so with reverence; and like that
greater Teacher who, thirteen hundred years
later, was to preach the self-same doctrine of
personal sacrifice, one may suppose that the
Pharaoh suffered a very Agony as he realised
that his principles were leading him to the loss
of all his dearest possessions. His restless

Letter from Ribaddi to the King of Egypt, reporting the progress of the rebellion under Aziru.

(British Museum, No. 29,801.)

generals in Egypt, eager to march into Syria, must have brought every argument to bear upon him; but the boy would not now turn back. "Put up thy sword into his place," he seems to have said; "for all they that take the sword shall perish with the sword."

4. THE FIGHTING IN SYRIA BECOMES GENERAL.

At this time the King of Byblos was one named Ribaddi, a fine old soldier who was loyal to Egypt in his every thought and deed. He wrote to Akhnaton urging him to send troops to relieve the garrison of Simyra, upon which Aziru was again pressing close; for if Simyra fell, he knew that Byblos could not for long hold out. Presently we find that Zimrida, the king of the neighbouring port of Sidon, has opened his gates to Aziru, and has marched with him against Tyre. Abimilki, the King of Tyre, at once wrote to Akhnaton asking for assistance; but on receiving no reply he, too, appears to have thrown in his lot with Aziru. Ribaddi was now quite isolated at Byblos; and from the beleaguered city he wrote to the Pharaoh telling him that "Simyra is like a bird in a snare." Akhnaton made no reply; and in a short time Ribaddi wrote again, saying, "Simyra, your fortress, is now in the power of the Khabiri."

These Khabiri were the Beduin from behind Palestine, who were being used as mercenaries by Aziru, and who themselves were making small conquest in the south on their own behalf. Thus the southern cities of Megiddo, Askalon, Gezer, and others, write to the Pharaoh asking for aid against them. Exasperated, however, by Akhnaton's inaction, Askalon and Gezer, together with the city of Lachish, threw off the Egptian yoke and attacked Jerusalem, which was still loyal to Egypt, being held by an officer named Abdkhiba. This loyal soldier at once sent a despatch to Akhnaton, part of which read as follows :—

> The King's whole land, which has begun hostilities with me, will be lost. Behold the territory of Seir, as far as Carmel, its princes are wholly lost; and hostility prevails against me. . . . As long as ships were upon the sea the strong arm of the King occupied Naharin and Kash, but now the Khabiri are occupying

the King's cities. There remains not one prince to my lord, the King; every one is ruined. . . . Let the King take care of his land, and . . . let him send troops. . . . For if no troops come in this year, the whole territory of my lord the King will perish. . . . If there are no troops in this year, let the King send his officer to fetch me and my brothers, that we may die with our lord, the King.

To this letter the writer added a postscript addressed to Akhnaton's secretary, with whom he was evidently acquainted. "Bring these words plainly before my lord the King," runs this pathetic appeal. "The whole land of my lord, the King, is going to ruin."

The letters sent to Akhnaton from the few princes who remained loyal form a collection which even now moves the reader. To Akhnaton they must have been so many sword-thrusts, and one may picture him praying passionately for strength to set them aside. Soon it would seem that the secretaries hardly troubled to show them to him; and ultimately they were so effect-ually pigeon-holed that they have only recently been discovered. The Pharaoh permitted himself to answer some of them, and seems to have

asked questions as to the state of affairs; but
never does he offer any encouragement. Lapaya,
one of the princes of the south, who had evidently received a communication from Akhnaton
in which his fidelity was questioned, wrote saying that if the Pharaoh ordered him to drive a
sword of bronze into his heart he would do so.
It is a commentary upon the veracity of the
Oriental that in subsequent letters this prince is
stated to have attacked Megiddo, and ultimately
to have been slain while fighting against the
Egyptian loyalists.

Addudaian, a king of some unknown city of
south Judea, acknowledges the receipt of a letter
from Akhnaton in which he was asked to remain
loyal; and he complains, in reply, of the loss of
various possessions. Dagantakala, the king of
another city, writes imploring the Pharaoh to
rescue him from the Khabiri. Ninur, a queen
of a part of Judea, who calls herself Akhnaton's
handmaid, entreats the Pharaoh to save her,
and records the capture of one of her cities by
the Khabiri.

And so the letters run on, each telling of some

disaster to the Egyptian cause, and each voicing the bitter complaint of those who were being sacrificed to the principles of a king who had grasped the meaning of civilisation too soon.

5. AZIRU AND RIBADDI FIGHT TO A FINISH.

Meanwhile Ribaddi was holding Byblos valiantly against Aziru's armies, and many were the despatches which he sent to Akhnaton asking for assistance against Aziru. Nothing could have been easier than the despatch of a few hundred men across the Mediterranean to the beleaguered port, and the number which Ribaddi asks for is absurdly small. Akhnaton, however, would not send a single man, but instead wrote a letter of gentle rebuke to Aziru, telling him to come to the City of the Horizon to explain his conduct. Aziru wrote at once to one of Akhnaton's courtiers who was his friend, telling him to speak to the Pharaoh and to set matters right. He explained that he could not leave Syria at that time, for he must remain to defend Tunip against the Hittites. The reader, who has seen the letter written by the governor of Tunip asking for help against Aziru, will realise the perfidy of this Amorite, who was now, no doubt, preparing to capture Tunip for the sake of its riches, and, having done so, would tell Akhnaton that he had entered it to hold it against the Hittites.

Akhnaton then wrote to Aziru insisting that he should rebuild the city of Simyra, which he had destroyed ; but Aziru again replied that he was too busy in defending Egyptian interests against the inroads of the Hittites to give his attention to this matter for at least a year. To this Akhnaton sent a mild reply ; but Aziru, fearing that the letter might contain some matter which it would be better for him not to hear, contrived to evade the messenger, and the despatch was brought back to Egypt. He wrote to the Pharaoh, however, saying that he would see to it that the cities captured by him should continue to pay tribute as usual to Egypt.

The tribute seems to have reached the City of the Horizon in correct manner until the last years of the reign,[1] though probably it was much less in quantity than had been customary. There was general confusion in Syria, as we have seen; but, as in the case of the struggle between Aziru and Ribaddi, where both professed their loyalty to Egypt, so, in all the chaos, there was a make-believe fidelity to the Pharaoh. The tribute was thus paid each year by a large number of cities, and it was probably not till the seventeenth and last year of Akhnaton's reign that this pretence of loyalty was altogether discarded.

In desperate straits at Byblos, Ribaddi made a perilous journey to the neighbouring city of Beyrût in order to attempt to collect reinforcements. No sooner had he left, however, than an insurrection occurred at Byblos, and Ribaddi paid for his loyalty to Egypt by losing the support of his own subjects. Presently Beyrût surrendered to Aziru, and Ribaddi was forced to fly. After many an adventure the stout old

---

[1] The reception of the tribute recorded in the tomb of Meryra II. (see page 170), although dated in the twelfth year of the reign, may represent a later event, since six daughters are shown in the scene; and it is not likely that the sixth daughter was born before the fifteenth year. Perhaps the date is a misreading or miswriting, influenced by that given in the tomb of Huya.

Q

king managed to regain control of Byblos, and
to set about the further defence of the city.

Meanwhile Aziru had paid a rapid visit to
Egypt, partly to justify his conduct and partly,
no doubt, to ascertain the condition of affairs
on the Nile. With Oriental cunning he managed to satisfy Akhnaton that his intentions
were not hostile to Egypt, and so returned to
the Lebanon. Ribaddi, hearing of this, at once
sent his son to the City of the Horizon to ex-
pose Aziru's perfidy and to plead for assistance
against him. At the same time he wrote to
Akhnaton a pathetic account of his misfortunes.
Four members of his family had been taken
prisoners; his brother was constantly conspir-
ing against him; old age and disease pressed
heavily upon him. All his possessions had been
taken from him, all his lands devastated; he
had been reduced by famine and the privations
of a long siege to a state of utter destitution,
and he could not much longer hold out. "The
gods of Byblos," he writes, "are angry with me
and sore displeased; for I have sinned against
the gods, and therefore I do not come before my
lord the King." Was his sin, one wonders, the

adoption for a while of Akhnaton's faith? To this communication Akhnaton seems to have made no reply.

6. AKHNATON CONTINUES TO REFUSE TO SEND HELP.

The messengers who arrived at the City of the Horizon of Aton, dusty and travel-stained, to deliver the many letters asking for help, must have despaired indeed when they observed the manner in which the news was received. Hateful to these hardy soldiers of the empire were the fine quays at which their galleys moored; hateful the fair villas and shaded avenues of the city ; and thrice hateful the rolling hymns to the Aton which came to them from the temple halls as they hurried to the Pharaoh's palace. The townspeople smiled at their haste in this city of dreams; the court officials delayed the delivery of their letters, scoffing at the idea of urgency in the affairs of Asia; and finally these wretched documents, written—if ever letters were so written—with blood and with tears, were pigeon-holed in the city archives and utterly forgotten save by Akhnaton himself. Instead of the brave music of the drums and bugles of the relieving army which these messengers had hoped to muster, there rang in their maddened ears only the ceaseless chants of the priestly ceremonies and the pattering love-songs of private festivals. Newly come from the sweat and the labour of the road, their brains still racked with the horror of war and yet burning with the vast hopes of empire, they looked with scorn at the luxury of Egypt's new capital, and heard with disgust the dainty tales of the flowers. The lean, sad-eyed Pharaoh, with his crooked head and his stooping shoulders, would speak only of his God; and, clad in simple clothes unrelieved by a single jewel, there was nothing martial in his appearance to give them hope. From the beleaguered cities which they had so lately left there came to them the bitter cry for succour; and it was not possible to drown that cry in words of peace, nor in the jangle of the systrum or the warbling of the pipes. Who, thought the waiting messengers, could resist that piteous call: "Thy city weeps, and

her tears are flowing"? Who could sit idle in
the City of the Horizon when the proud empire,
won with the blood of the noblest soldiers of
the great Thothmes, was breaking up before their
eyes? What mattered all the philosophies in
the world, and all the gods in heaven, when
Egypt's great dominions were being wrested from
her? The splendid Lebanon, the white kingdoms
of the sea, Askalon and Ashdod, Tyre and Sidon,
Simyra and Byblos, the hills of Jerusalem, Kadesh
and the great Orontes, the fair Jordan, Tunip,
Aleppo, the distant Euphrates. . . . What counted
a creed against these? God? The truth? The
only god was He of the Battles, who had led
Egypt into Syria; the only truth the doctrine
of the sword, which had held her there for so
many years.

Looking back across these thirty-two centuries,
can one yet say whether the Pharaoh was in the
right, or whether his soldiers were the better
minded? On the one hand there is culture,
refinement, love, thought, prayer, goodwill, and
peace; on the other hand, power, might, health
hardihood, bravery, and struggle. One knows
that Akhnaton's theories were the more civilised, the more ideal; but is there not a pulse

which stirs in sympathy with those who were
holding the citadels of Asia? We can give our
approval to the ideals of the young king, but
we cannot see his empire fall without bitterly
blaming him for the disaster. Yet in passing
judgment, in calling the boy to account for the
loss of Syria, there is the consciousness that
above our tribunal sits a judge to whom war
must assuredly be abhorrent, and in whose
eyes the struggle of the nations must utterly
lack its drama. Thus, even now, Akhnaton
eludes our criticism, and but raises once more
that eternal question which as yet has no
answer.

7. AKHNATON'S HEALTH GIVES WAY.

It is possible that the Pharaoh now realised
his position, and one may suppose that he tried
as best he could to pacify the turbulent princes
by all the arts of diplomacy. It does not seem,
however, that he yet fully appreciated the catas-
trophe which was now almost inevitable — the
complete loss of Syria. He could not bring
himself to believe that the princes of that

country would play him false; and he could have had no idea that he was being so entirely fooled by such men as Aziru. But when at last the tribute ceased to come in regularly, then, too late, he knew that disaster was upon him.

The thoughts which now must have held sway in his mind could not have failed to carry him down the dark steps of depression to the very pit of despair, and one may picture him daily cast prone upon the floor before the high altar of the Aton, and nightly tossing sleepless upon his royal bed. It seems that he had placed great reliance upon a certain official, named Bikhuru, who was acting as Egyptian commissioner in Palestine; but now it is probable that he received news of that unfortunate personage's flight, and later of his murder.[1] Then came the report that Byblos had fallen, and one is led to suppose that that truly noble soldier Ribaddi did not survive the fall of the city which he had so tenaciously held. The news of the surrender of other important Egyptian strongholds followed rapidly, and still there came the pathetic appeal for help from the minor posts which yet held out.

[1] Breasted : History, p. 388.

Akhnaton was now about twenty - eight years
of age, and already the cares of the whole world
seemed to rest upon his shoulders.   Lean and
lank was his body; his face was thin and lined
with worry; and in his eye one might, perhaps,
have seen that hunted look which comes to those
who are dogged by disaster.   It is probable that
he now suffered acutely from the distressing
malady to which he was a victim, and there
must have been times when he felt himself
upon the verge of madness.   His misshapen
skull came nigh to bursting with the full
thoughts of his aching brain, and the sad knowledge that he had failed must have pressed upon
his mind like some unrelenting finger.   The
invocations to the Aton which rang in his head
made confusion with the cry of Syria.   Now he
listened to the voices of his choirs lauding the
sweetness of life; and now, breaking in upon the
chant, did he not hear the solemn voices of his
fathers calling to him from the Hills of the West
to give account of his stewardship?   Could he
then find solace in trees and in flowers?   Could
he cry " Peace " when there was red tumult in
his brain?

His moods at this time must have given cause for the greatest alarm, and his behaviour was, no doubt, sufficiently erratic to render even those nobles who had so blindly followed him mistrustful of their leader. In a frenzy of zeal in the adoration of the Aton, Akhnaton now gave orders that the name of all other gods should suffer the same fate as that of Amon, and should be erased from every inscription throughout the land. This order was never fully carried out; but one may still see in the temples of Karnak, Medinet Habu, and elsewhere, and upon many lesser monuments, the chisel marks which have partially blurred out the names of Ptah, Hathor, and other deities, and have obliterated the offending word "gods."

The consternation which this action must have caused was almost sufficient to bring about a revolution in the provinces, where the old gods were still dearly loved by the people. The erasing of the name of Amon had been, after all, a direct war upon a certain priesthood, and did not very materially affect any other localities than that of Thebes. But the suppression of the numerous priesthoods of the many deities who held sway throughout Egypt threw into disorder the whole country, and struck at the heart not of one but of a hundred cities. Was the kindly old artificer Ptah, with his hammer and his chisel, to be tumbled into empty space? Was the beautiful, the gracious Hathor—the Venus of the Nile—to be thrown down from her celestial seat? Was it possible to banish Khnum, the goat-headed potter who lived in the caves of the Cataract, from the life of the city of Elephantine; the mysterious jackal Wepwat from the hearts of the men of Abydos; or the ancient crocodile Sebek from the ships and the fields of Ombos? Every town had its local god, and every god its priesthood; and surely the Pharaoh was mad who attempted to make war upon these legions of heaven. This Aton, whom the king called upon them to worship, was so remote, so infinitely above their heads. Aton did not sit with them at their hearth - side to watch the kettle boil; Aton did not play a sweet - toned flute amongst the reeds of the river; Aton did not bring a fairy gift to the new - born babe. Where was the sacred tree in whose branches one might hope to see him seated? —

where was the eddy of the Nile in which he
loved to bathe?—and where was the rock at
whose foot one might place, as a fond offering,
a bowl of milk? The people loved their old
gods, whose simple ways, kind hearts, and
quick tempers made them understandable to
mortal minds. But a god who reigned alone
in solitary isolation, who, more remote even
than the Jehovah of the Hebrews, rode not
upon the clouds nor moved upon the wings of
the wind, was hardly a deity to whom they
could open their hearts. True, the sunrise and
the sunset were the visible signs of the godhead;
but let the reader ask any modern Egyptian
peasant whether there is aught to stir the
pulses in these two great phenomena, and he
will realise that the glory of the skies could not
have appealed particularly to the lesser subjects
of Akhnaton, who, moreover, were not permitted
to bow the knee to the flaming orb itself. When
the Christian religion took hold of these peas-
ants, and presented for their acceptance the same
idea of a remote though loving and considerate
God, it was only by the elevation of saints and
devils, angels and powers of darkness, almost to

the rank of demigods, that the faith prospered.
But Akhnaton allowed no such tampering with
the primary doctrine, and St George and all
the saints would have suffered the erasure of
their very names.

8. AKHNATON'S LAST DAYS AND DEATH.

The troubles which Akhnaton by such actions
gathered around himself, while disturbing to his
adherents, must have given some degree of
pleasure to those nobles who saw in the king's
downfall the only hope of Egypt.   Horemheb,
the commander-in-chief of the inactive armies,
could now begin to prepare himself against the
time when he should lead a force into Syria
to restore Egyptian prestige.   Tutankhaton,
betrothed to Akhnaton's third daughter, could
dream of the days when he would make himself
Pharaoh, and carry the court back to glorious
Thebes.   Even Meryra, the High Priest of
Aton, seems to have allowed his thoughts to
drift away from the City of the Horizon
wherein the sun of Egypt's glory had set, for

it does not seem that he ever made use of the
tomb there prepared for him.   These last stages
of Akhnaton's life must thus have been embittered by a doubt of the sincerity of his
closest friends, and by the knowledge that, in
spite of all their protestations, he had failed to
plant "the truth" in their hearts.

The queen had borne him no son to succeed to
the throne, and there appeared to be nobody
to whom he could impart what he felt to be
his last instructions.   There can be no question
that he was still greatly loved by those who
surrounded his person, but there were few who
hoped that his religion, so disastrous to Egypt,
would survive him.   In this extremity Akhnaton
turned to a certain noble, probably not of royal
blood, whose name seems to have been Smenkhkara, though some have read it Saakara.[1]   Nothing
is known regarding his previous career, but one
may suppose that he appeared to Akhnaton to
be the least unreliable of his followers.   To him
the king imparted his instructions, revealing all
that words could draw from his teeming brain.

---

[1] It is doubtful whether the second sign is *menkh* or *àà*, they
being somewhat alike.

The little Princess Merytaton, now but twelve years of age, was called from her games, and with pomp and ceremony was married to this Smenkhkara, thus making him the legitimate heir to the throne, Merytaton being the eldest daughter and sole heiress of the Pharaoh.

Feeling that his days were numbered, Akhnaton then associated Smenkhkara upon the throne with him as co-ruler, and was thus able to familiarise the people with their future lord. In later years, after Akhnaton's death, Smenkhkara was wont to write after his name the words "beloved of Akhnaton," as though to indicate that his claim to the throne was due to Akhnaton's affection for him, as well as to the rights derived from his wife.

But what mattered the securing of the succession to the throne when that throne had been shaken to its very foundations, and now seemed to be upon the verge of utter wreck? Akhnaton could no longer stave off the impending crash, and from all sides there gathered the forces which were to overwhelm him. His government was chaotic. The plotting and scheming of the priests of Amon showed signs of coming to a successful issue. The anger of the priesthoods of the other gods of Egypt hung over the palace like some menacing storm-cloud. The soldiers, eager to march upon Syria as in the days of the great Thothmes III., chafed at their enforced idleness, and watched with increasing restlessness the wreck of the empire.

Now through the streets of the city there passed the weary messengers of Asia hurrying to the palace, no longer bearing the appeals of kings and generals for support, but announcing the fall of the last cities of Syria and the slaughter of the last left of their rulers. The scattered remnants of the garrisons staggered back to the Nile at the heels of these messengers, pursued to the very frontiers of Egypt by the triumphant Asiatics. From the north the Hittites poured into Syria; from the south the Khabiri swarmed over the land. As the curtain is rung down on the turbulent scene, one catches a glimpse of the wily Aziru, his hands still stained with the blood of Ribaddi and of many another loyal prince, snatching at this city and trampling on that. At last he has cast aside his mask, and with the tribute which had been promised to Egypt he now, no doubt, placates the ascending Hittites, whose suzerainty alone he admits.

The tribute having ceased, the Egyptian treasury soon stood empty, for the government of the country was too confused to permit of the proper gathering of the taxes, and the working of the gold-mines could not be organised. Much had been expended on the building of the City of the Horizon, and now the king knew not where to turn for money. In the space of a few years Egypt had been reduced from a world power to the position of a petty state, from the richest country known to man to the humiliating condition of a bankrupt kingdom.

Surely one may picture Akhnaton now in his last hours, his jaw fallen, his sunken eyes widely staring, as the full realisation of the utter failure of all his hopes came to him. He had sacrificed Syria to his principles; but the sacrifice was of no avail, since his doctrines had not taken root even in Egypt. He knew now that the religion of the Aton would not outlive him, that the knowledge of the love of God was not yet to be made known to the world. Even at this moment the psalms of the Aton were beating upon his ears, the hymns to the God who had forsaken him were drifting into his palace with the scent of the flowers; and the birds which he loved were singing as merrily in the luxuriant gardens as ever they sang when they had inspired a line in the king's great poem. But upon him now there had fallen the blackness of despair, and already the darkness of coming death was closing around him. The misery of failure must have ground him down as beneath the very mountains of the west themselves, and the weight of the knowledge of all that he had lost could not be borne by his enfeebled frame.

History tells us only that, simultaneously with the fall of his empire, Akhnaton died; and the doctors who have examined his body report that death may well have been due to some form of stroke or fit. But in the imagination there seems to ring across the years a cry of complete despair, and one can picture the emaciated figure of this "beautiful child of the Aton" fall forward upon the painted palace-floor and lie still amidst the red poppies and the dainty butterflies there depicted.

VIII.

THE FALL OF THE RELIGION OF AKHNATON.

"Thus disappeared the most remarkable figure in early Oriental history. . . . There died with him such a spirit as the world had never seen before."—BREASTED : 'History of Egypt.'

---

1. THE BURIAL OF AKHNATON.

THE body of Akhnaton was embalmed in the city which he had founded ; and while these mortal parts of the great idealist were undergoing the lengthy process of mummification, the new Pharaoh Smenkhkara made a feeble attempt to retain the spirit of his predecessor in the new *régime.* Practically nothing is known of his brief reign, but it is apparent from subsequent events that he entirely failed to carry on the work of Akhnaton, and the period of his sovereignty is marked by a general tendency to abandon the religion of the Aton. Smenkhkara had dated the first year of his reign from the day of his accession as co-ruler with Akhnaton, and thus it is that there are no inscriptions found which record his first year, although there are many references to his second year. The main event must have occurred some three months after the commencement of his sole reign, when the body of Akhnaton was carried in solemn state through the streets of the city and across the desert to the tomb which had been made for him in the distant cliffs.

The mummy had been wrapped, as was usual, in endless strips of linen; and amongst these there was placed upon the royal breast a necklace of gold, and over the face an ornament cut in flat gold foil representing a vulture with wings outstretched—a Pharaonic symbol of divine protection. In many burials of this dynasty a vulture such as this was placed upon the mummy; and representations of an exactly similar ornament are shown in the tombs of Sennefer and others at Thebes. It is somewhat surprising that the body of Akhnaton, who was so averse to all old customs, should thus have this royal talisman upon it ; and it would seem that some of the strict rules of the Aton worshipper had already been relaxed by his successor. Akhnaton had retained but three of the ancient divine symbols, so far as one can tell from the reliefs and paintings— namely, the uræus or cobra, the sphinx, and the hawk, which were often used as ornaments. But one may ask whether the vulture had really been dispensed with by him. It is true that he banned the vulture - hieroglyph in the inscriptions, as we have already seen on the outer coffin of Queen Tiy ;[1] but his reason for so doing was that by such a hieroglyph the name of the goddess Mut was called to mind, and that goddess, being the consort of Amon, was not to be tolerated. The vulture which was laid upon the mummy, however, had nothing to do with Mut, nor had it any likeness to the hieroglyph. It was originally a representation of the presiding genius of Upper Egypt, and corresponded to the uræus, which primarily represented the power of Lower Egypt. It is true, again, that it was the custom for the

[1] Page 187.

Pharaohs to be shown in the sculptures and paintings with this vulture hovering in protection over their heads, and that Akhnaton seems to have dispensed with such a symbol. But this was perhaps due to the fact that the disk and rays, symbolic of Aton, had taken its place above the royal figure. There is no reason, after all, to suppose that this form of vulture was absolutely banned, since the uræus and the hawk were retained;[1] and though, as will presently be seen, it will be natural to think that it was placed on Akhnaton's mummy at his successor's suggestion, there is nothing to show that Akhnaton himself did not desire it to be laid there.

Over the linen bandages on the body there were placed ribbons of gold foil encircling the mummy — probably around the shoulders, the middle, and the knees,—joined to other ribbons running the length of the body at the back and front. These ribbons were inscribed with Akhnaton's name and titles, and thus recorded for all time the identity of the mummy to which

---

[1] The scarab, another symbol from older times, seems to have been retained, for a gold heart-scarab is said to have been found in Akhnaton's tomb.—Petrie: History of Egypt, ii. 220.

they adhered. Money being somehow found, the body was wrapped in sheets of pure gold, sufficiently thin to be flexible, and was placed in a splendid coffin, designed in the usual form of a recumbent figure, and inlaid in a dazzling manner with rare stones and coloured glass. Down the front of this coffin ran a simple inscription, the hieroglyphs of which were also inlaid. It read: "The beautiful prince, The Chosen One of Ra, the King of Upper and Lower Egypt, living in Truth, Lord of the Two Lands, Akhnaton, the beautiful child of the living Aton, whose name shall live for ever and ever." [1] There is one curious feature about this inscription. When Akhnaton made the outer coffin for his mother, in or about the twelfth year of his reign, he was particularly careful not to use the hieroglyph representing the goddess Maat when writing the word *maat*, "truth." But this sign is employed now upon his own coffin; and one can only presume, therefore, that the coffin was made after Akhnaton's death, and that the new Pharaoh Smenkh-

---

[1] In Egytian: Ḥeq nefer, Rå setept, Seten bati, Ȧnkh em Måȧt, Neb taui, Akhnaton, Pa sherȧ nefer en Pa Aton ånkh, enti åuf ånkhu ren ḥeḥ zet. This was all that was written upon the coffin.

kara had not the same objection to the representation of the goddess as had his predecessor. We may now better understand the presence of the vulture symbol also; for it is obvious that before Akhnaton's funeral had taken place his strict *régime* had been relaxed.

The royal mummy was now carried to its tomb and there deposited, together with such funeral furniture and offerings as were considered necessary. The four alabaster canopic jars, always conspicuous in an Egyptian burial, were here not wanting. The stopper of each jar was exquisitely carved to represent the head of Akhnaton, wearing the usual male wig of the period, and having the royal cobra upon the forehead. From these heads one sees that the art of Akhnaton was modified immediately after his death, and its more pronounced characteristics were already being toned down. This slackening in the rules which Akhnaton had made shows us how entirely dependent the movement had been upon its leader; and we realise the more clearly how strong a character was his. Ere even the king's burial had taken place the death of his religion was assured.

2. THE COURT RETURNS TO THEBES.

Smenkhkara died, or was deposed, about a year after Akhnaton's death. He was succeeded by another noble, Tutankhaton,[1] who, in order to legitimise his accession, obtained in marriage Akhnaton's second daughter Ankhsenpaaton, a girl barely twelve years old. Thus Smenkh-kara's wife, Merytaton, became a dowager-queen at the age of thirteen or so, and her little sister took her place upon the throne.

By this time the priests of Amon had begun to hold up their heads once more, and to scheme for the downfall of Aton with renewed energy. Pressure was soon brought to bear on Tutankhaton, and he had not been upon the throne more than a year or so when he was persuaded to consider the abandonment of the City of the Horizon and his return to Thebes. He did not yet turn entirely from the religion of the Aton, but attempted to take a middle course between the two factions, giving full

---

[1] Probably he is to be identified with Tutu, a well-known noble of this period—the words ankhaton, "Living in Aton," being added to make the name more majestic.

licence both to the worshippers of the Aton and to those of Amon. Horemheb, the commander-in-chief of the idle army, seems to have been one of the leaders of the reactionary movement. He did not concern himself so much with the religious aspect of the question: there was as much to be said on the one side as on the other. But it was he who knocked at the doors of the heart of Egypt and urged the nation to awake to the danger in Asia. For him there were no scruples as to warfare, and the doctrine of the sword found favour in his sight. An expedition was fitted out, and the reigning Pharaoh was persuaded to lead it. Thus we read that Horemheb was "the companion of his Lord upon the battlefield on that day of the slaying of the Asiatics." [1] Akhnaton had dreamed of the universal peace which still is a far-off wraith to mankind; but

---

[1] See note on page 67. This inscription is found on the door-posts of the tomb of Horemheb, which, by the greatly increased titles, were set up some time after the rest of the tomb was finished, and thus probably in the reign of Tutankhaton. A fragment of gold-leaf has recently been found showing this king in his chariot charging Asiatic enemies. The present writer recently found part of a shrine of his in the desert on the road to the gold mines. See 'Travels in the Upper Egyptian Deserts' (Blackwood).

Horemheb was a practical man in whom that dream would have been but weakness which was such mighty strength in the dead king.

The new Pharaoh now changed his name from Tutankhaton to Tutankhamon, and, to the sound of martial music, returned to Thebes. The City of the Horizon was left to its fate, and it was not long before the palaces and the villas became the home of the jackals and the owls, while the temples were partly pulled down to provide stone for other works. However much the reigning Pharaoh differed in views from Akhnaton, it would not have been possible to leave the royal body lying in sight of this wreck of all the hopes that had been his. Akhnaton, moreover, was Tutankhamon's father-in-law, and it was only through the rights of Akhnaton's daughter that the Pharaoh held the throne. His memory was still regarded with reverence by many of his late followers, and there could be no question of leaving his body in the deserted city. It was therefore carried to Thebes in its coffin, together with the four canopic jars, and was placed, for want of a proper sepulchre, in the tomb of Queen Tiy, which had been reopened for the purpose.

Tutankhamon showed the trend of his policy by both restoring the temple of the Aton at Karnak and at the same time repairing the damage done by Akhnaton to the works of Amon. The style of art which he favoured was a modified form of Akhnaton's method, and the influence of his movement is still apparent in the new king's work. He did not reign long enough, however, to display much originality, and after a few years he disappears, almost unnoticed, from the stage. On his death the question of inviting Horemheb to fill the vacant throne must have been seriously considered, but there was another candidate in the field. This was Akhnaton's father-in-law, Ay, who had been one of the most important nobles in the group of courtiers at the City of the Horizon. It was he who had sheltered Queen Nefertiti before she had passed into Akhnaton's palace, and it was in his tomb that the great hymn to the Aton was inscribed. He had been loudest in the praises of the preacher king and of his doctrines, and he still retained the title " Father-in-law " as his most cherished designation.

Religious feeling at this time was running high, for the partisans of Amon and those of

Aton seem still to have been struggling for the supremacy, and Ay appeared to have been regarded as the most likely man to bridge the gulf between the two factions. A favourite of Akhnaton, and still tolerant of all that was connected with the late movement, he was not averse to the cult of Amon, and by conciliating both parties he managed to obtain the throne for himself. His power, however, did not last for long, and as the priests of Amon regained the confidence of the nation at the expense of the worshippers of the Aton, so the prestige of Ay declined. His past relationship to Akhnaton, which even as king he carefully recorded within his cartouche, now told against him rather than for him, and about eight years after the death of Akhnaton he disappeared like his predecessors.

3. THE REIGN OF HOREMHEB.

There was now no question who should succeed. All eyes were turned to Horemheb, who had already almost as much power as the Pharaoh. The commander - in - chief at once ascended the throne, and was received by the populace with the utmost rejoicings. At this time there was living at Thebes the Princess Nezemmut, the sister of Akhnaton's Queen Nefertiti, and hence the daughter of Dushratta, King of Mitanni. Owing to previous inter-marriages between the royal house of Egypt and that of Mitanni, both Nefertiti and Nezemmut were descendants of Pharaohs of the Eighteenth Dynasty. Nezemmut had come to Egypt early in the reign of Akhnaton, and later had perhaps married some Egyptian nobleman; but she was now a widow, and had recently been appointed to the post of "Divine Consort," — that is to say, High Priestess—of Amon. As she was probably the younger sister of Nefertiti, she may have been about six years of age when Nefertiti was married to Akhnaton at the age of eight. Hence she would have been about twenty-three at his death, and would now be just over thirty.

To this princess, as representing both the rights of the old line of Pharaohs and those of the god Amon, without the now condemning close relationship to Akhnaton which characterised the other existing royal princesses, Horemheb was at once married. The religion of the Aton was now fast disappearing. In a tomb dating from the third year of Horemheb's reign, the words "Ra whose body is Aton" occur; but this is the last mention of the Aton, and henceforth Amon-Ra is unquestionably supreme. A certain Pa-atonemheb, who had been one of Akhnaton's favourites, was at about this time appointed High Priest of Ra-Horakhti at Heliopolis, and thus the last traces of the religion of the Aton were merged into the Heliopolitan theology, from which that religion at the beginning had emanated.

The neglected shrines of the old gods once more echoed with the chants of the priests throughout the whole land of Egypt. Inscriptions tell us that Horemheb "restored the temples from the pools of the Delta marshes to Nubia. He fashioned a hundred images . . . with all splendid and costly stones. He established for them daily offerings every day. All the vessels of their temples were wrought of silver and gold. He equipped them with priests and with ritual priests, and with the choicest of

The Temple at Luxor.

the army. He transferred to them lands and cattle, supplied with all necessary equipment." By these gifts to the neglected gods Horemheb was striving to bring Egypt back to its natural condition; and with a strong hand he was guiding the country from chaos to order, from fantastic Utopia to the solid old Egypt of the past. He was, in fact, the preacher of sanity, the very apostle of the Normal.

He led his armies into the Sudan, and returned with a procession of captive chieftains roped before him. He had none of Akhnaton's qualms regarding human suffering, and these unfortunate prisoners are seen to have their arms bound in the most cruel manner. Finding the country to be lawless he drafted a number of stern laws, and with sound justice administered his kingdom. Knowing that Syria could not long remain quiet, he organised the Egyptian troops, and so prepared them that, but a few years after his death, the soldiers of the reigning Pharaoh were swarming once more over the lands which Akhnaton had lost.

272 THE FALL OF THE RELIGION OF AKHNATON.

4. THE PERSECUTION OF AKHNATON'S MEMORY.

The priests of Amon-Ra had now begun openly to denounce Akhnaton as a villain and a heretic, and as they restored the name of their god where it had been erased, so they hammered out the name and figure of Akhnaton wherever they saw it. Presently they pulled down the Aton temple at Karnak, and used the blocks of stone in the building of a pylon for Amon-Ra. Soon it was felt that Akhnaton's body could no longer lie in state, together with that of Queen Tiy, in the Valley of the Tombs of the Kings. The sepulchre was therefore opened once more and the name "Akhnaton" was everywhere erased from the inscriptions, as was his figure from the scenes upon the shrine of Queen Tiy. The mummy was lifted from its coffin and the royal name was cut out of the gold ribbons which passed round it, both at the back and the front. It was then replaced in the coffin, and from this the name was also erased.

The question may be asked why it was that the body was not torn to pieces and scattered to the four winds, since the king was now so fiercely hated. The Egyptians, however, entertained a peculiar reverence for the bodies of their dead, and it would have been a sacrilege to destroy the mummy even of this heretic. No thought could be entertained of breaking up the body upon which the divine touch of kingship had fallen: that would have been against all the sentiments which we know the Egyptians to have held. The cutting out of the name of the mummy was sufficient punishment: for thereby the soul of the king was debarred from all the benefits of the earthly prayers of his descendants, and became a nameless outcast, wandering unrecognised and unpitied through the vast underworld. It was the name "Akhnaton" which was hated so fiercely; and one may perhaps suppose that the priests would have been willing to substitute the king's earlier name, Amonhotep, upon the mummy had they been pressed to do so. His name and figure as Amonhotep IV. is not damaged upon the monuments; but only the representations of him after the adoption of the name Akhnaton have been attacked.

S

The tomb, polluted by the presence of the heretic, was no longer fit for Tiy to rest in; and the body of the queen was therefore carried elsewhere, perhaps to the sepulchre of her husband Amonhotep III. The shrine, or outer coffin, in which her mummy had lain was pulled to pieces, and an attempt was made to carry it out of the tomb to its owner's new resting-place, but this arduous task was presently abandoned, and one portion of the shrine was left in the passage, while the rest remained in sections in the burial-chamber. Some of the queen's toilet utensils which had been buried with her were also left, probably by mistake. The body of Akhnaton, his name taken from him, was now the sole occupant of the tomb. The coffin in which it lay rested upon a four-legged bier some two feet or so from the ground, and in a niche in the wall above it stood the four canopic jars. And thus, with a curse, the priests left their great enemy. The entrance of the tomb was blocked with stones, and sealed with the seal of the necropolis; and all traces of its mouth were hidden by rocks and *débris*.

The priests would not now permit the name of Akhnaton to pass a man's lips, and by the end of the reign of Horemheb, the unfortunate boy was spoken of in official documents as "that criminal." Not forty years had passed since Akhnaton's death, yet the priesthood of Amon was as powerful as it had ever been at any period of its existence. There were still living men who had been old enough at the time of the Aton power to grasp its doctrines; and those same eyes which had looked upon the fair City of the Horizon might now disturb the creatures of the desert in the ruined courts where the grave boy-Pharaoh had presided so lately. These men joined their voices to that crowd of priests who, not daring to allow the word Akhnaton to form itself upon their lips, poured curses upon the excommunicated and nameless "criminal." Through starry space their execrations passed, searching out the wretched ghost of the boy, and banning him, as they supposed, even in the dim uncertainties of the Lands of Death. Over the hills of the west, up the stairs of the moon, and down into the caverns under the world, the poor twittering shadow was hunted and chased by the relentless magic of the men whom he had tried to reform. There was no place for his memory upon earth, and in the under-world the priests denied him a stone upon which to lay his head. It is not easy now to realise the full meaning to the Egyptians of the excommunication of a soul: cut off from the comforts of human prayers; hungry, forlorn, and wholly desolate; forced at last to whine upon the outskirts of villages, to snivel upon the dung-heaps, to rake with shadowy fingers amidst the refuse of mean streets for fragments of decayed food with which to allay the pangs of hunger caused by the absence of funeral-offerings. To such a pitiful fate the priests of Amon consigned "the first individual in history"; and as an outcast amongst outcasts, a whimpering shadow in a place of shadows, the men of Thebes bade us leave the great idealist, doomed to the horrors of a life which will not end, to the misery of a death that brings no oblivion.

5. THE FINDING OF THE BODY OF AKHNATON.

Thus, sheathed in gold, the nameless body lay, while the fortunes of Egypt rose and fell and the centuries slid by. A greater teacher

than Akhnaton arose and preached that peace
which the Pharaoh had foreshadowed, and soon
all Egypt rang with the new gospel.   Then
came the religion of Muhammed, and the days
of the sword returned.   So the years passed,
and many a wise man lived his life and disappeared; but the first of the wise men of
history lay undiscovered in the heart of the
Theban hills.

Now it happened that there was a fissure in
the rocks in which the sepulchre was cut, and
during the rains of each season a certain amount
of moisture managed to penetrate into the
chamber.   This gradually rotted the legs of the
bier upon which Akhnaton's body lay, and at last
there came a time when the two legs at the head
of the coffin gave way and precipitated the royal
body on to the ground.   The bandages around
the mummy had already fallen almost to powder,
and this jerk sent the golden vulture which was
resting upon the king's face on to his forehead,
where it lay with the tail and claws resting over
the left eye-socket of the skull.   Presently the
two remaining legs of the bier collapsed, and
the whole coffin fell to the ground, the lid being

partly jerked off, thus revealing the king's head at one end and his feet at the other, from all of which the flesh had rotted away.

In January 1907 the excavations in the Valley of the Tombs of the Kings which were being conducted by Mr Theodore Davis, of Newport, Rhode Island, U.S.A., on behalf of the Egyptian Government, brought to light the doorway of the tomb, and it was not long before an entrance was effected. A rough stairway led down into the hillside, bringing the excavators[1] to the mouth of the passage, which was entirely blocked by the wall which the priests had built after they had entered the tomb to erase Akhnaton's name. Beyond this wall the passage was found to be nearly choked with the *débris* of the three earlier walls, the first of which had been built after Queen Tiy had been buried here, the second after Akhnaton's agents had entered the tomb to erase the name of Amon, and the third after Akhnaton's body had been laid beside that of his mother. On top of this heap of stones lay the

---

[1] The present writer assisted at the opening of this tomb. A full account of the find will be published by Mr Davis, and therefore only a brief description, already published with Mr Davis's permission in article form, must be given here.

side of the funeral shrine of the queen which the priests had abandoned after attempting to carry it out with her mummy. In the burial-chamber beyond, the remaining portions of this shrine were found. Upon these one saw the figures of Akhnaton and his mother worshipping beneath the rays of the Aton. The inscriptions showed the erasure of the name of Amonhotep III., and the substitution in red ink of that king's second name, Nebmaara; and one observed that at a later date the name and figures of Akhnaton had been hammered out.

At one side lay the coffin of Akhnaton, as it had fallen from the bier. The name of Akhnaton upon the coffin had been erased, but was still readable; and the gold ribbons from which his name had been cut out still encircled the body, back and front. The golden vulture lay as has been described above, and the necklace still rested on the breast, while the whole decaying body was found to be wrapped in sheets of gold. In a recess above this coffin stood the canopic jars, and in another part of the tomb Queen Tiy's toilet utensils were found, from one of which the name of Amonhotep III. had been erased.

The bones, when examined by Dr Elliot Smith, F.R.S., were found to be those of a young man of not more than about twenty-eight years of age,—that is to say, the age at which Akhnaton has been shown in the above pages to have died. The skull was pronounced to be that of a man who suffered from epileptic fits, and who was probably subject to hallucinations. Curiously enough, the idiosyncrasies of this mis-shapen skull are precisely those which Lombroso has stated to be so usual in a religious reformer. The face had crumbled away, but the lower jaw was intact; and when this was placed in position one could see at once the great resemblance to the well-known portraits of Akhnaton which had survived the wreck of his city.

There could thus be no doubt that the mummy of this wonderful Pharaoh had at last been found; but since Akhnaton had always been thought, though without particular reason, to have been a much older man, the identity was questioned. It was suggested that the body was perhaps that of Smenkhkara, the successor of Akhnaton, which by some error had managed to be placed in Akhnaton's coffin. But how, then, did the gold ribbons inscribed with Akhnaton's name manage to be placed around the body? And apart from the extreme improbability that the mummy which was thus labelled with Akhnaton's name, and which lay in his coffin, should be that of any other king but Akhnaton, one may ask in this case how it is that the body has the well-known physical characteristics of the great heretic if it be that of Smenkhkara, who was not related to the king?

It has been stated that the presence of the vulture upon the body is against the identification with Akhnaton. This has already been shown to be capable of explanation; but it may here be noted that if Smenkhkara would not have placed the vulture upon Akhnaton's body, then by the same token the mummy is not likely to be that of Smenkhkara, and there is certainly no other prince of this period with whom to identify the body. In conclusion, it may be added that of all the royal mummies now known there is not one which can be so clearly shown to belong to the Pharaoh with whom it has been identified as this mummy can be 'shown to belong to Akhnaton. The body was lying in a coffin inscribed with Akhnaton's name; it was bound round with ribbons inscribed with his name; it had the physical characteristics of the portraits of Akhnaton; it had the idiosyncrasies of a religious reformer such as he was; it was that of a man of Akhnaton's age as deduced from the monuments; it lay in the tomb of Akhnaton's mother; those who had erased the names must have thought it to be Akhnaton's body, unless one supposes an utter chaos of cross-purposes in their actions; and finally, there is nobody else who, with any degree of probability, it could be.

Thus one may say that, without the vaguest shadow of a doubt, the body of this the most remarkable figure of early Oriental history has been brought to light; and with this assurance we may close this sketch of his life, which has been written partly for the purpose of thus explaining the significance of Mr Davis's great discovery, and partly to introduce the general reader to one of the most interesting characters ever known. In this brief outline it has only been possible to touch upon the main char-

acteristics which the few remaining inscriptions
and monuments seem to reveal; but to the
most casual reader it will be apparent that
there stands before him a personality of surprising vigour and amazing originality, and one
deserving of careful study.   In an age of superstition, and in a land where the grossest poly-
theism reigned absolutely supreme, Akhnaton
evolved a monotheistic religion second only to
Christianity itself in purity of tone.   He was
the first human being to understand rightly
the meaning of divinity.   When the world
reverberated with the noise of war, he preached
the first known doctrine of peace ; when the
glory of martial pomp swelled the hearts of
his subjects, he deliberately turned his back
upon heroics.   He was the first man to preach
simplicity, honesty, frankness, and sincerity ;
and he preached it from a throne.   He was
the first Pharaoh to be a humanitarian; the
first man in whose heart there was no trace of
barbarism.   He has given us an example three
thousand years ago which might be followed
at the present day: an example of what a
husband and a father should be, of what an

honest man should do, of what a poet should feel, of what a preacher should teach, of what an artist should strive for, of what a scientist should believe, of what a philosopher should think. Like other great teachers he sacrificed all to his principles, and thus his life plainly shows — alas! — the impracticability of his doctrines; yet there can be no question that his ideals will hold good "till the swan turns black and the crow turns white, till the hills rise up to travel, and the deeps rush into the rivers."

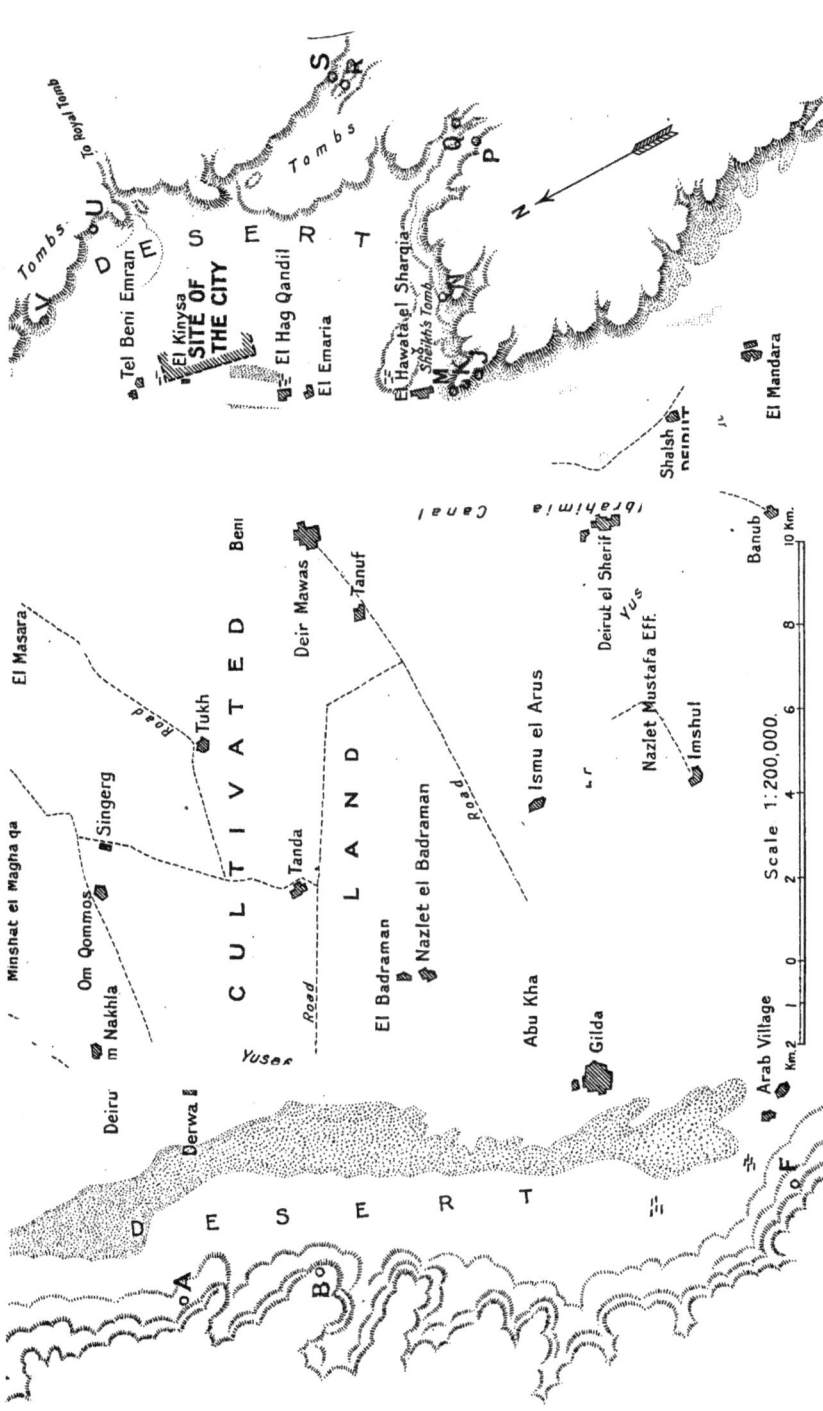

NOTE: Of the Boundary Stelae only those lettered A, B, F, J, K, M, N, P, Q, R, S, U, V and X, still remain. The position of these is shown upon the Map.

FROM THE CAIRO SCIENTIFIC JOURNAL.

SURVEY DEP. CAIRO 1909 (151)

INDEX.

Aahmes I., 7

Abdkhiba, governor of Jerusalem, appeal of, to Akhnaton for help, 236

Adonis, connection of, with Aton, 15, 37, 49, 136 *et seq.*

Akhnaton, personality of, 2—ancestors of, 7 *et seq.*—birth of, 42 *et seq.*—change of name from Amonhotep to, 45 note, 91 *et seq.*—marriage of, 53 —accession of, 58 *et seq.*—first years of the reign of, 62 *et seq.*—new city founded by, 88 *et seq.*—site of the city selected by, 92 *et seq.*—foundation ceremonies performed by, 94 *et seq.*—departure of, from Thebes, 105 *et seq.*—age of, 110 *et seq.*—religion of Aton formulated by, 115 *et seq.*—tenth to twelfth years of the reign of, 149 *et seq.* — similarity of the hymn of, to Psalm civ., 155 *et seq.* —representations of, in his palace, 167 *et seq.*—historical events of tenth to twelfth years of the reign of, 169 *et seq.*—thirteenth to fifteenth years of the reign of, 189 *et seq.*—name of Amon obliterated by, 193 *et seq.*—affection of, for his family, 208 *et seq.*—friends of, 213 *et seq.*—troubles of, 217 *et seq.*—last two years of the reign of, 223 *et seq.*—conscientious objections of, to warfare, 226 *et seq.* —health of, gives way, 246 *et seq.*—last days and death of, 252—fall of the religion of, 258 *et seq.* — burial of, 258—body of, brought to Thebes, 266—persecution of the memory of,

272 *et seq.*—finding of the body of, 276 *et seq.*—ideals of, 283

Amon or Amon-Ra, worship of, 12—priesthood of, 20, 45 *et seq.*, 77—break with the priesthood of, 88 *et seq.*—Akhnaton obliterates the name of, 193 *et seq.* — restoration of the worship of, 272 *et seq.*

Amonhotep I., 7

Amonhotep II., 10

Amonhotep III., "the Magnificent," 11, 13, 28, 33 *et seq.*, 49, 54—death of, 57, 111—second name of, 186, 187, 195

Amonhotep IV.: see Akhnaton

Amonhotep-son-of-Hapu, the "wise man," 33

Animal worship, 18 *et seq.*

Ankhsenpaaton, third daughter of Akhnaton, birth of, 109—marriage of, 112, 264

Apis, the sacred bull, worship of, 16, 87

Apiy, letter to Akhnaton from, 85

Art, the new style of, 68 *et seq.*, 101

Aswan, commemoration tablet at, 107 —statue of Amonhotep III. at, *ib.*

Aton, the name, 37, 92 and note—rise of, 45 *et seq.*—development of the religion of, 76 *et seq.*—nature of the religion of, 84 *et seq.*—founding of new city for the worship of, 88 *et seq.* —religion of, formulated, 115 *et seq.*—connections of the worship of, with older religions, 135 *et seq.* —hymns of the worshippers of, 149 *et seq.*—Meryra made high priest of,

THE END.

www.ingramcontent.com/pod-product-compliance
Lightning Source LLC
Chambersburg PA
CBHW040149270326
41929CB00035B/3361